To Be Like Jesus

GWEN R. SHAW

Engeltal Press
P. O. Box 447
Jasper, ARK 72641-0447

Printed in the United States of America

CONTENTS

Page

Foreword i

Introduction ii

My Throne Room Experience 1

John Chapter 1 - Full of Grace and Truth 4

John Chapter 2 - The True Sons of the Father are Generous and Extravagant in Their Giving 12

John Chapter 3 - The Son of the Father is Born Again by the Holy Spirit 16

John Chapter 4 - The True Sons of the Father Will Worship the Father in Spirit and Truth 20

John Chapter 5 - The Father's Work Never Ceases — Nor Does Ours 23

John Chapter 6 - The Sons of God Have Been Sealed by the Holy Spirit 48

John Chapter 7 - Obedience to God Will Help to Keep You From Error 51

John Chapter 8 - The Sons of God Know From Whence they Came 53

John Chapter 10 - The Father Knows His Children and Loves Them 68

John Chapter 11 - When We Live Right, God Always Hears Our Prayers 85

John Chapter 12 - "Where I Am, There Shall Also My Servant Be" 86

John Chapter 13 - "Going Home" 90

John Chapter 14 - Our Father's House 94

John Chapter 15 - Honour the Root Out of Which You Have Come 104

John Chapter 16 - Prepare For Persecution 113

John Chapter 17 - God Honours Those Who Honour Him 121

John Chapter 18 - Accept Your Suffering Out of the Hand of the Father and It Will Give You Strength 128

Luke and Matthew - Jesus Speaks to the Father While Hanging on the Cross .130

John Chapter 20 - The First Call to Women to Proclaim the Glad Message of the Resurrection Was Given as Jesus Was Ascending to the Father 133

Conclusion 136

Scriptures 142

FOREWORD

You are holding in your hand a book that has been in my heart for twenty-five years. I have lived by the truths that are written on these pages.

I can take no credit for them; it is the Father Who made these truths real to my heart through the Holy Spirit.

It all began during a week of fasting when I visited the Throne Room of God while in prayer in January, 1971.

I was living alone at that time, and had much more time to pray and meditate, so the Lord and I became very close companions. Except for one or two friends, He was the only one I had to talk with.

I have spent many hours in The Gospel According to St. John. It is my favourite book in the Bible because it draws me so close to my Saviour.

But it is also a mirror of what the Lord expects of me, and what I too expect of myself. Sad to say, I don't always live up to its idealism. But I know that it is the perfect picture of what every child of God should be when he is born again of the Spirit of God, and puts on Christ.

It was the truths in this book that inspired me to write the little Gospel Chorus which so many of you have learned to love:

Let the love of my God shine through me;
Let the beauty of Jesus men see;
Let the pattern of the Son
Be the one, the only one
That men will see in me.

I am convinced that the deepest desire of all of our hearts is that we might be like Jesus.

Gwen R. Shaw

INTRODUCTION

To Be Like Jesus

"Following Christ is not an outward imitation, since it touches man at the very depths of his being.

Being a follower of Christ means becoming conformed to Him Who became a servant, even to giving Himself on the cross (see Philippians 2:5-8)[1]*. Christ dwells by faith in the heart of the believer (Ephesian 3:17)*[2]*, and thus the disciple is conformed to the Lord. This is the effect of grace, of the active presence of the Holy Spirit in us.*

Having become one with Christ, the Christian becomes a member of His body, which is the Church (1 Corinthians 12:13, 27)[3]*.*

By the work of the Spirit, baptism radically configures the faithful to Christ in the paschal mystery of death and resurrection; it 'clothes him' in Christ (Galatians 3:27)[4]*.*

'Let us rejoice and give thanks,' exclaims St. Augustine, speaking to the baptized, 'For we have become not only Christians, but Christ...Marvel and rejoice: We have become Christ!'"

Pope John Paul II

[1]**Philippians 2:5-8**, *"Let this mind be in you, which was also in Christ Jesus: Who, being in the form of God, thought it not robbery to be equal with God: But made himself of no reputation, and took upon him the form of a servant, and was made in the likeness of men: And being found in fashion as a man, he humbled himself, and became obedient unto death, even the death of the cross."*

[2]**Ephesians 3:17**, *"That Christ may dwell in your hearts by faith; that ye, being rooted and grounded in love...."*

[3]**1 Corinthians 12:13**, *"For by one Spirit are we all baptized into one body, whether we be Jews or Gentiles, whether we be bond or free; and have been all made to drink into one Spirit."*

1 Corinthians 12:27, *"Now ye are the body of Christ, and members in particular."*

[4]**Galatians 3:27**, *"For as many of you as have been baptized into Christ have put on Christ."*

My Throne Room Experience

During the first week of January, 1971, I was fasting and praying in Chicago. During that time the Lord took me into His Throne Room. He showed me my place in the family of God. He told me that I was as precious to Him as His Son, Jesus. This gave me a tremendous desire and longing in my heart to be like Jesus, to think like He thought, to desire what He desired, to live like He lived, to love like He loved, to be pure in my spirit like He was, and just to be like Him in every way that it was humanly possible.

I had difficulty understanding this, so He told me to study the relationship between His Son Jesus, and Himself, as it is revealed in the Gospel of St. John. He instructed me to put myself in Jesus' place every time that He spoke of His relationship with His Father. In this book I have chosen to write only from these particular portions of the Gospel where Jesus speaks of His relationship which He had with His Father.

The Lord showed me that I needed to recognize how close He and I also were to each other, and that, as I studied this relationship as it is revealed through John's writing, I would understand, not only my privileges, as His "Son," His mature Son, but also my duties, responsibilities, and all that is expected of me — for maturity makes demands upon one who is the heir of the Father.

"*NOW* ARE WE THE SONS OF GOD!"

Too often, when we read in the Scriptures about our being joint-heirs with Christ, we assume it is a transaction and responsibility which will take place sometime in the future. But this is not true. We are NOW His sons, even though it is quite impossible to see all that this implies and entails. Even the benefits of our relationship with the Father are not realized to the full at this present time.

Because John had the revelation of our position in the Father's family, he could write, *"Beloved, now are we the sons of God, and it doth not yet appear what we shall be: but we know that, when he shall appear, we shall be like him; for we shall see him as he is"* (1 John 3:2).

But John not only saw both our present and future position, he also exhorted us as to how we attain unto that high calling, when he said, *"And every man that hath this hope in him purifieth himself, even as he is pure"* (1 John 3:3).

Our position is so much higher and greater than what we have conceived. St. Augustine caught a glimpse of it when he so daringly said, "We have become Christ!" And Pope John Paul courageously dares to echo an affirmative "AMEN!"

For most Christians (both Catholics and Protestants) this revelation is almost too much for our minds to grasp. That is because we still dwell in the "child-stage" of being a Christian, and have not grown up into the maturity and spiritual strength, which alone can prepare us for Throne Room revelation and transformation.

Adulthood brings responsibility. A boy-child cannot give seed, nor can a girl-child produce ovum, so as long as we remain in the child-stage spiritually, we cannot reproduce after our kind. Is this why Christ has not been formed in so many of us? Are we in a state of immaturity? Are we perpetual spiritual teen-agers?

Paul saw this great lack in the Church of the Galatians when he said, *"My little children, of whom I travail in birth again until Christ be formed in you"* (Galatians 4:19).

Paul knew that Christians, in their infant stage, do not have the Christ-image nor Christ-character. That has to be developed through experience and relationship — and that takes time. Sometimes Christians, through wrong influence (as happened in the case of the Galatians, who listened to erroneous teachings) can even regress, rather than progress in their spiritual development.

And then there are others who, because of their teachable hearts and gentle spirits, develop much more quickly than others. A knowledge of the Word of God, the indwelling Presence of the Holy Spirit, and a great love for God, are the three things that help one to grow into mature sons of God.

The purpose of this study is to search out the Scriptures. We cannot take time to search out the entire Bible, but we will study about this son-and-Father relationship in the Book that the Father told me to use for my personal understanding on this subject, i.e. The Gospel of St. John.

John Chapter One

FULL OF GRACE AND TRUTH

JOHN 1:14, "*And the Word was made flesh, and dwelt among us, (and we beheld his glory, the glory as of the only begotten of the Father), full of grace and truth.*"

Jesus was "full of grace and truth." In order for us to even begin to live and walk in this Father-son relationship, we need the same attributes that Jesus had. We need to be filled with His grace and truth. We need to have the courage to be honest with ourselves. If we lie to ourselves and live a life of pretense, we will never be able to accept correction, nor learn the higher laws of Heaven. Many stumble right here at the beginning. They find it too difficult to be honest with themselves. They don't like what they see in their hearts. Their own conscience convicts them of their misdeeds and lack of Christlike character, but they do not want to deal with it, so they turn away from truth. And when they do that, they turn into darkness because they are turning away from Him Who is the Truth.

But in order to accept truth (which is often painful), we need that measure of grace that enables us to face the truth about ourselves and also to be able to love others when we know the truth about them.

Why can I go to Jesus with all my sins and shortcomings, and know that He will receive me, and still love me? Is it not because I know that He has this grace?

John Newton(1725-1807), the former wicked slave dealer, had a great revelation on the infinite Grace of God when he wrote his immortal hymn, *"Amazing Grace."*

It is easy to imagine Jesus having this wonderful grace, but if I am to be like Jesus, then it is expected of me, that I too will be a vessel of grace — grace for grace (John 1:16).

You may be saying, "But Sister Gwen, you are expecting too much of me."

In reply I say, read John 1:16, *"And of his fulness have all we received, and grace for grace."*

The nature of man is one of demanding perfection in others, judging and criticizing all who fail, and pride in our own accomplishments. Many of us still live under The Law given by Moses; we have not been transformed into the Christ-life of grace and truth. John said, "*For the law was given by Moses, but grace and truth came by Jesus Christ*" (John 1:17). It is Grace and Truth that made the New Covenant so much better and greater than the Old Covenant.

Pope John Paul II says, "To imitate and live out the love of Christ is not possible for man by his own strength alone. He becomes capable of this love only by virtue of a gift received." We flee to the Father to receive this gift of love and grace through the Holy Spirit.

As long as we have the spirit of judging we are living by the Law of Moses. This Law does not put the Spirit of Christ in us, rather it edifies the spirit of Moses, i.e. the Law. But when we live by the nature of Christ, through the indwelling Presence of the Holy Spirit, we live on a much higher plane, even the same on which Jesus lived.

Paul said to the Galatians, "*Now I say, That the heir, as long as he is a child, differeth nothing from a servant, though he be lord of all; But is under tutors and governors until the time appointed of the father. Even so we, when we were children, were in bondage under the elements of the world: But when the fulness of the time was come, God sent forth his Son, made of a woman, made under the law, To redeem them that were under the law, that we might receive the adoption of sons. And because ye are sons, God hath sent forth the Spirit of his Son into your hearts, crying, Abba, Father. Wherefore thou art no more a servant, but a son; and if a son, then an heir of God through Christ*" (Galatians 4:1-7).

Israel was God's family. But as long as they were under the Law, they were in the School of Discipline. They were learning to do what was right, and were restricted from doing what was wrong. The things they were taught were good, but knowing what is right and wrong does not change the nature of man, nor does it perfect him (Hebrews 9:9; 10:1).

As long as they were in training, they lived the same restricted lives that servants live. But when the Fullness of Time came, God sent His Son, born of a woman who was trained under the Law, an observant Jewess. By His sacrificial death, the Laws and Ordinances, which condemned man (because he never really was able to truly live by them) were nailed to the Cross, and man was set free forever. Paul writes to the Colossians, "*And you, being dead in your sins and the uncircumcision of your flesh, hath he quickened together with him, having forgiven you all trespasses, Blotting out the handwriting of ordinances that was against us, which was contrary to us, and took it out of the way, nailing it to his cross*" (Colossians 2:13-14).

Having accomplished that great sacrifice of compassion and mercy, Jesus cried out from the cross, *"IT IS FINISHED!"* From then on, all who came to Him for forgiveness were adopted as sons, and received the Spirit of God's Son into their hearts, enabling them to rightfully call God, "Abba Father."

We who came to Him no longer sat in the schoolroom with the slave children, but became heirs of God. We didn't have to be taught what is right and wrong. We had His nature imparted to us. We became "possessed" by the Spirit of Christ.

On the mission field I have seen people who have become possessed of demon spirits. It has changed their nature, their personality, their way of thinking and doing things. Sometimes the evil spirits take such complete control of the person, and the change is so powerful and awful that he has to be committed to a mental asylum. We have seen cases where the evil spirit takes dominion over the spirit of the man he possesses, and causes the man to do very evil things even to those whom he loves.

If evil spirits can do these things, cannot the Spirit of Christ also take over a life, control it, inspire it, bless it and do good for it?

THE SON REVEALS THE FATHER TO THE WORLD

John 14:9, *"When Jesus was with His disciples in the Upper Room He said to Philip, 'Have I been so long time with you, and yet hast thou not known me, Philip? He that hath seen me hath seen the Father; and how sayest thou then, Shew us the Father?'"*

To all of His disciples He said, "*If ye had known me, ye should have known my Father also: and from henceforth ye know him, and have seen him*" (John 14:7).

The word "declared" is *exegeomai*(1834) in Greek. It means, "to tell, lead forward, to bring out, declare thoroughly and particularly." From this verb comes the English word "exegesis," "the unfolding through teaching."

If it is true that through the new birth and the indwelling Presence of the Holy Spirit I am in the image of Christ, and that Christ, through His character and His teachings, portrayed and revealed the Father, then I, by my life, will do the same. People will see the Father in me.

I TOO COME FROM THE BOSOM OF GOD

JOHN 1:18, "*No man hath seen God at any time; the only begotten Son, which is in the bosom of the Father, he hath declared him.*"

Because I have been born again by the Holy Spirit, through the new birth I too come from the bosom of the Father.

The closer you are to anyone, the greater revelation you have about that person, as you get to know him better. It is believed that John knew the Lord Jesus better than any of the apostles because he lay with his head on the Lord's bosom (John 13:23). It is this intimacy with the Lord that qualified John to write with the greatest depth of understanding of the Father-son relationship, as it is revealed to us in the Gospel According to St. John. It also qualified him to write the judgments of Revelation. For it is wrong to speak about the judgment of God in a spirit of anger or hatred. If one cannot talk about judgment with tears, one should not talk about it at all.

Because of our Father-son relationship with our God, we are qualified to present Him to the world.

THE TRUE SON OF THE FATHER WILL LIVE A CONSTANT SPIRIT-FILLED LIFE

JOHN 1:33-34, *"And I knew him not: but he that sent me to baptize with water, the same said unto me, Upon whom thou shalt see the Spirit descending, and remaining on him, the same is he which baptizeth with the Holy Ghost. And I saw, and bare record that this is the Son of God."*

John the Baptist was told by the Father that He would be able to recognize the Messiah by a certain sign: That sign was very unusual, the Holy Spirit would come down upon Him and remain with Him. When this happened John said, "*I saw, and bare record that this is the Son of God.*"

All of Christ's followers have the Holy Spirit, for without Him they could not be brought to the Lord. But the beautiful thing about Jesus is that the Holy Spirit remained on Him.

This is the sign by which we can identify true "sons of God." They are constantly filled with the Holy Spirit. They live the overcomer's life. They are not up one day and down the next. Happy in Jesus one day, and depressed another day. Some Christians live such defeated lives that no one wants to be around them. They are grumpy, angry, argumentative, disrespectful, factious, impolite, discourteous, rebellious, rude, sullen, troublemakers. Their pastors feel their negative vibrations when they step into the church. People avoid them. Their families are embarrassed by them, and the Holy Spirit is grieved by their conduct because He knows the reproach this so-called Child of God is bringing upon His Lord, and himself.

John could easily identify the true Son because of the witness of the Holy Spirit. The Holy Spirit remained on the Son. The true son of the Father will bear this same witness to the world and the Church — He will constantly live a Spirit-filled life. And thereby all the world will bear witness that he is a son of God.

THE SONS OF GOD CAN RECOGNIZE OTHER SONS OF GOD

JOHN 1:47, *"Jesus saw Nathanael coming to him, and saith of him, Behold an Israelite indeed, in whom is no guile!"*

John 2:24-25, "But Jesus did not commit himself unto them, because he knew all men, And needed not that any should testify of man: for he knew what was in man."

Not all your suspicions are of the devil! It could easily be that what you are feeling is from the Holy Spirit. The children of the Father are warned by the Father to beware of what is in the hearts of men. The Father takes care of His own, and He protects them by a still, small voice. Sometimes that "voice" can be such a soft whisper that it is easy to ignore it and pretend that you never heard it at all.

Jesus recognized Nathanael as a true Israelite (a son of the Prince), in whom there was nothing false.

Sad to say, many Christians still have the traits of their former lives; they are scheming, deceptive, tricky and cheating. Everything they do, even the good things they do, are tainted by these negative traits and sins. Because Jesus was pure, Nathanael could also recognize who He was; he said, *"Rabbi, thou art the Son of God; thou art the King of Israel"* (John 1:49).

Jesus was recognized as the true Son of the Father because of His understanding of others, and His ability to find them in the Spirit.

John Chapter Two

THE TRUE SONS OF THE FATHER ARE GENEROUS AND EXTRAVAGANT IN THEIR GIVING

JOHN 2:6-7, "*And there were set there six waterpots of stone, after the manner of the purifying of the Jews, containing two or three firkins apiece. Jesus saith unto them, Fill the waterpots with water. And they filled them up to the brim.*"

It was nearing the end of the wedding feast when the hosts ran out of wine. They only needed a little more to satisfy everyone, when Mary brought the need to the attention of her Son. At first He pretended to be indifferent to their need. This was because He did not want to draw attention to Himself, which He knew would happen if He were to openly perform a miracle right there and then. But seeing the look of expectation in her eyes, He could not refuse her, so He commanded, *"Fill the pots with water."*

How much wine did that make? According to the estimation of Bible scholars it would have made between 120 to 180 gallons, depending on the size of the stone pots (A firkin measures nine/ten gallons.). That was enough wine to intoxicate everyone in Cana! It reveals the generous nature of our Lord. He does not hold back in His giving. As the song writer wrote, "He giveth and giveth and giveth again!" (Annie Johnson Flint).

As children of the Father, and with our Elder Brother Jesus as our example, we hereby learn the lesson on how to give. There is no room for stinginess in the heart of a son of God. If you find your hand holding fast to your possessions, and your heart unwilling to share with others the things that the Lord has given you, you do not have the Spirit of Christ in you.

The area in which we are tested in this is through tithing. Many are not willing to give the Lord their tithes. They make all kinds of excuses, such as "tithing is for the Old Testament, it is not for the Christians." But this is only an excuse. A true son of the Father will give *"pressed down, shaken together and running over,"* — and count it all joy. Jesus was not only generous, He was extravagant! He was what some men might call "wasteful."

The same was true when He fed the five thousand. He multiplied the loaves and fishes so generously that there were many baskets of bread left over. Always make enough for one more person, you never know when Elijah will knock at your door. You may find yourself entertaining angels unaware.

THE SONS OF GOD WILL NEVER MAKE A PROFIT OUT OF ANOTHER MAN'S SEARCH FOR GOD

JOHN 2:15-16, *"And when he* [Jesus] *had made a scourge of small cords, he drove them all out of the temple, and the sheep, and the oxen; and poured out the changers' money, and overthrew the tables; And said unto them that sold doves, Take these things hence; make not my Father's house an house of merchandise."*

After witnessing the generosity and liberality of the Son of God, it is easy to understand why He was so angry when He saw the greed of man in His Father's House. Everything Jesus did, He did out of the loving kindness of His heart. So it grieves Him deeply when He sees the greedy money changers and traders. The reason these people were permitted to be there was because of at least two factors:

1. When the worshippers came to the Tabernacle they brought sacrifices to offer to God. Many of the people had come from far away, some even had travelled many weeks by ship from other lands to get there. It would have been very difficult for them to bring an animal from so far away. And even if they attempted to do so, it would probably have been injured or become sick on the way, and therefore would not have been accepted to be the perfect sacrifice.

The greedy traders took advantage of this, and because of their greed and love of money they took advantage of the people. Besides, there was so much corruption that the rabbis who inspected the animals, would have deliberately tried to find something wrong with them. They no doubt had a secret agreement with the dealers so that they would get a percentage of the profit. They charged exorbitant prices for the sacrificial animals, and everyone made a profit — except the worshipper. He was cheated by the high cost of the sacrifice.

2. The money changers had a very important transaction to make because the Law of Moses had forbidden them to make any manner of graven image, the likeness of any human, beast, fowl, crawling reptile, or fish (Deuteronomy 4:15-19). The money used in Israel at that time had the image of a Roman emperor or some other important person. Therefore, in the eyes of the Jews, it was a sin to use it in connection with the worship in the Temple. It could not be used to buy the sacrificial offerings. It had to be exchanged for acceptable temple-money first. The exchange rate was very high. The people were cheated twice, once in the exchange, and the second time by the purchase of the high priced sacrificial oxen, sheep and doves.

It was not so much because of the sale of the animals and the exchange of the money that the Son was angry with them, it was the way in which they did it. Jesus saw the spirits of greed and cheating and dishonesty. He saw the rich making themselves richer and the poor becoming poorer because of the greed of the rich. And it was all done in the name of religion.

The Son was grieved to see men profiting by the desire of the people to obey and worship God.

No son of God will take advantage of the man or woman who is hungry for God. He will never seek to make a profit out of anyone's search for the Lord. Yet it has happened all through the ages. The religious leaders have sheared the sheep and slaughtered the lambs (Ezekiel 34).

Jesus grieved over the situation. He remembered Ezekiel had prophesied about this. For a short while Jesus stepped into what will one day be His position of authority during the Millennium when He shall reign as King of kings and Priest of priests.

If we are true children of the Father we will never be permitted to take advantage of God's people to our own profit. Many have done it in the Church. And it has grieved the heart of the Father, and brought His wrath upon them. The day will soon come when He will overturn their tables and free their "oxen, sheep and doves." And when that happens miracles will happen, as they did then. *"The blind and the lame came to him in the temple; and he healed them. And ...the chief priests and scribes saw the wonderful things that he did, and the children crying in the temple, and saying, Hosanna to the Son of David..."* (Matthew 21:14-15).

John Chapter Three

THE SON OF THE FATHER IS BORN AGAIN BY THE HOLY SPIRIT

JOHN 3:5-7, "*Jesus answered, Verily, verily, I say unto thee, Except a man be born of water and of the Spirit, he cannot enter into the kingdom of God. That which is born of the flesh is flesh; and that which is born of the Spirit is spirit. Marvel not that I said unto thee, Ye must be born again.*"

In order to become the son of God, one must be reborn by the Holy Spirit. When we were born of our earthly father and mother we received their likenesses, mannerisms and genes. But when we were born again of the Holy Spirit we received the same identities and attributes from our Heavenly Father. They were imparted into our spirits by the indwelling Presence of the Holy Spirit in our lives.

You became a citizen of the country wherein you were born, unless the laws of the land stated otherwise. When I was born again by the Holy Spirit, I became a citizen of the Kingdom of God. I am loyal to my "country." I love it and want to live in it all of my life and for eternity. I speak the language of my natural country and of my spiritual "country."

Anyone who does not have this born-again experience only has a religious feeling, and not a change of nature. There is a big difference.

WE HAVE BECOME A NEW CREATION

JOHN 3:31, "*He that cometh from above is above all: he that is of the earth is earthly, and speaketh of the earth: he that cometh from heaven is above all.*"

When we are born again of the Spirit we experience a new birth which qualifies us to become Citizens of Heaven. We are seated in Heavenly Places and have communion with others of like mind. We can then say that we, like Jesus, have come from above. No more do we belong to the earth, no more do we speak about or love earthly things, for *"old things have passed away, behold, all things have become new."* We have become a new creation (2 Corinthians 5:17). We have a new God-given authority.

THE SON OF GOD IS A TRUE WITNESS WHO SPEAKS GOD'S WORD IN THE FULL ANOINTING OF THE HOLY SPIRIT, YET IN SPITE OF THAT HE IS NOT ALWAYS ACCEPTED NOR BELIEVED.

JOHN 3:32, 34, "*And what he hath seen and heard, that he testifieth; and no man receiveth his testimony. For he whom God hath sent speaketh the words of God: for God giveth not the Spirit by measure unto him.*"

Because of the dramatic change in our lives we will lose many of our old friends. Somehow the holy and the profane do not mix any better than oil and water. Our new way of talking and walking cramps the life-style of our old acquaintances. Friends who once loved to chat with us for hours, now begin to avoid us. We don't talk about the same things anymore.

Nor do we seem to long for that old life. We are now no longer of the world and the love of the world is not in us. John had this complete change of life; that is why he wrote to the Church, "*Love not the world, neither the things that are in the world. If any man love the world, the love of the Father is not in him*" (1 John 2:15).

BECAUSE THE FATHER LOVES ME HE HAS CONFIDENCE IN ME

JOHN 3:35, *Jesus said, "The Father loveth the Son, and hath given all things into his hand."*

Love inspires trust and faith. *Love... "believeth all things, hopeth all things, endureth all things*" (1 Corinthians 13:7).

The all-knowing Father would never have entrusted ALL THINGS into the hands of a Judas-christ. One day there will come on this earth an evil man who will pretend that he is the Christ. He will demand the obedience and worship of all men. He will seduce and deceive many (if possible even the elect), but the Father will never hand over the power of the Kingdom into his hands.

Only the True Son is honoured with the power and the Glory forever and ever. The Father placed the fullness of His strength and authority into His Son's care and keeping.

And because you are to the Father all that Jesus was to Him, He has put into your hands this same authority, so that it is true that *"The works that I do, shall ye do also"* (John 14:12).

Jesus said to His disciples as He sent them out on their missionary journey, "*Behold, I give unto you power to tread on serpents and scorpions, and over all the power of the enemy: and nothing shall by any means hurt you*" (Luke 10:19).

Oh, the love and the trust that are behind these words! He says the same to you as He did to His followers so long ago. Because He loves you, He has placed in your hands the power to heal the sick, and in your mouth the power to speak the command of life from the dead, and cast out demons. All power is given unto you. It is the Father's gift of love to His son whom He loves — even to you!

John Chapter Four

THE TRUE SONS OF THE FATHER WILL WORSHIP THE FATHER IN SPIRIT AND TRUTH

JOHN 4:21, 23-24, "*Jesus saith unto her, Woman, believe me, the hour cometh, when ye shall neither in this mountain, nor yet at Jerusalem, worship the Father...But the hour cometh, and now is, when the true worshippers shall worship the Father in spirit and in truth: for the Father seeketh such to worship him. God is a Spirit: and they that worship him must worship him in spirit and in truth.*"

No one has a better understanding of how to worship the Father than the Son. He knows every desire of His Father. When Jesus was in Heaven He saw how the angels worshipped the Father. It was a pure worship, full of truth and adoration. But when He came to earth He saw men's form of worship, and it grieved His heart.

Every true son of the Father who has been a Throne-Room saint, has difficulty in conforming to man's organized form of so-called "worship." He is so close to the Father that he knows it is not from the heart. Many, as they worship the Father, only do so as an outward show. Their minds are on other things even while they sing,

"Holy, Holy, Holy, Lord God Almighty!
All Thy works shall praise Thy name,
In earth, and sky, and sea;"

And oh, how it grieves the sons of the Father!

But the Father will have those who will worship Him in the Spirit and in purity and truth. They will be those who are His true sons, born of the Spirit.

One of the things that grieved the Son was that everyone thought their own way of worshipping the Father was the only right way. But Jesus said to the woman at the well, "*Woman, believe me, the hour cometh, when ye shall neither in this mountain, nor yet at Jerusalem, worship the Father.*"

He was saying that it was not the place, the Church, the Temple, nor the particular denomination that made the difference — it was the heart. Yet religious man has not heard the words of the Son. For two thousand years they have split and divided the Church into many fragments, each one thinking they alone have the truth. While it is true that they have the truth, they probably do not have ALL of it. May the Lord help us to find our brothers and sisters in the lives of those who worship the Father in a way that is different to us.

THE TRUE SON OF GOD LIVES TO DO THE WILL OF HIS FATHER AND BRING IN ALL OF THE HARVEST

JOHN 4:34, "*Jesus saith unto them, My meat is to do the will of him that sent me, and to finish his work.*"

Every good son will obey his father. He will seek to please him, help him carry his burden, assist him in his work, and honour him with absolute obedience. Obedience is a sign of respect. He will put the desire of his father ahead of his own.

There is no doubt that Jesus must have felt hungry when He saw His disciples returning with freshly-baked bread from the village. The smell of it must have made His mouth water. But there was a greater hunger in His heart than the hunger for natural food. It was the hunger to do His Father's will, and to finish His work.

When it is harvest time the true son will stay with the harvesters until long after the sun has set. He is so anxious to finish the harvesting of the grain that he refuses to stop and go to bed. He works until he is exhausted, because he knows that if the weather turns bad he may lose the harvest. He knows that his father's harvest is his harvest.

Jesus had the heart of a true Son. He sensed the awesome responsibility of soul-winning, because He knew that the night was coming when no man will be able to work, and the door of opportunity will be closed forever. For every nation, for every situation, we are only given brief "windows of opportunity."

That was the hour for Samaria. It was harvest time for the little nation within a nation. Not many years later, near the close of Jesus' ministry, when He was on His way back to Jerusalem to lay down His life, He wanted to stop in Samaria, but the people refused to let Him come into the village. Opposition had been raised up against him — probably by the Samaritan priests who were fearful of losing their control over the people. The opposition was so strong against Jesus that James and John wanted to call down fire from heaven to burn them up (Luke 9:51-56). There was just a small time slot for saving souls.

The true son of the Father will always be conscious of the hour in which he is living and working, and he will always seek to accomplish all that needs to be accomplished so that no souls would be lost who would have had opportunity to come to Christ.

We have many preachers and ministers, but few soul-winners. May the Lord bring us into mature sonship so that we can bring in the final harvest.

John Chapter Five

THE FATHER'S WORK NEVER CEASES — NOR DOES OURS

JOHN 5:17, "*But Jesus answered them, My Father worketh hitherto, and I work.*"

When Jesus was criticized by the religious rulers for healing the crippled man on the Sabbath, and telling him to pick up his bed and walk on the Sabbath day, he said to them, *"My Father worketh hitherto, and I work."*

Judaism emphasizes the importance of keeping the Sabbath free from any kind of work, or anything that resembles work, so when Jesus healed the sick man at the Pool of Bethesda, and told him to carry his mat away, they were angry. They were so concerned about keeping the Law of Moses that they could not rejoice at the Law of Grace, Truth, Love and Mercy.

Religion can make one very narrow-minded and cruel. It tries to force others into the same mould as we ourselves are in. We demand of others what we demand of ourselves. Religion does not necessarily bring us close to God, only devotion can do that. That is what Jesus meant when He said to the Woman of Samaria, "*But the hour cometh, and now is, when the true worshippers shall worship the Father in spirit and in truth: for the Father seeketh such to worship him*" (John 4:23).

Body worship is beautiful, for the body can express its love to God in the song, the dance, by the clapping of hands, the lifting up of hands, etc., but it is the deep worship of the soul and spirit of man, inspired by devotion to God, that brings one into intimacy with the Beloved. The Bride of Song of Solomon said, "*...the king hath brought me into his chambers: we will be glad and rejoice in thee, we will remember thy love more than wine*" (Song of Solomon 1:4).

How many times are we reminded that God finished His work in six days and rested on the seventh! We have heard this teaching so often that we have actually come to believe that, when God finished His work in six days, He rested on the seventh — and every day after that. As though, He went up to Heaven, sat down on His big throne, and hasn't done a stitch of work since then!

The Church fell into the same narrow-minded thinking when it began to believe that miracles stopped at the close of the early Church age. We were taught that when the apostles died, the gifts of the Spirit ceased with them. For almost 2000 years we have been taught by our Church scribes and professors that God doesn't heal the sick any more. Speaking in tongues went out of date with the death of the founders of the Church. And then we were taught that if miracles did take place, it was the devil who did them. I heard that lie during the early years of my Christian walk. Only more recently, as the move of God has swept the Church through the Charismatic Awakening, and the Scriptures have become available to the common layman, have we broken free from this error. At last we have learned that Jesus Christ is the same, yesterday, today and forever (Hebrews 13:8).

Jesus was telling the people that God has never stopped working — and neither has He. Jesus said, "*My Father works...and I work also.*" This is present tense. It is not past tense, nor future tense, it is a NOW tense. The

Father is working today. Jesus is working today. You and I, as sons and daughters of God, follow our Father's example in doing good works all the time. God only *rested* on the Sabbath — He did not retire! We also take our days of rest, but we do not retire from doing His work. He cannot stop! We dare not stop! Old age does not excuse us from the responsibility and the opportunity to serve.

When a man's sons grow up and become dependable, their father often takes them in as partners of the firm; one will read such signs as "Shaw and Sons Ltd." That means that the son is no longer just one of the workers in the business, rather, he is one of the "bosses." He is an owner, and has a share in the stock. He now takes on the responsibility of running the business, along with his father. If there is a loss, he shares the loss. If there is gain, he shares the profit. He does not "clock out" with the regular employees. He stays, often until the wee hours of the morning, and bears the burden of responsibility together with the father.

That is the way that our working relationship with our Father should be. We are no longer servants, we are joint-heirs with His Son. The Father has included my name in His title deed, Father and Sons! And I do my best to live up to that honour.

THE TRUE SON OF THE FATHER RECOGNIZES HIS IDENTITY AND THE GREATNESS THAT IT BESTOWS UPON HIM

JOHN 5:18, *"Therefore the Jews sought the more to kill him, because he not only had broken the sabbath, but said also that God was his Father, making himself equal with God."*

Only the son who hates his father could deny the relationship that is between them. Some sons hate their fathers so much that they call him "the old man." This is very degrading and dishonouring.

The world has suffered for centuries because there is so little true affection between fathers and sons.

Jesus taught us to pray, "*Our Father which art in Heaven...*" because He wanted the lonely, hurting world to know that they do have a Father, One who is not afar off; and that He loves them and cares for them.

When we call Jehovah our Father we are raising our status and confessing that we belong to the family of God. Today man says that he is a descendant of the ape. But when we have God in our hearts we can recognize our family pedigree.

You cannot go around claiming everyone as your father. It doesn't work that way. You have only one father. No one can have two biological fathers.

Men who are sons of great fathers, who have become famous by some important deed they have accomplished, or by their birth, are very proud to be identified with their fathers.

This is why the true son of God is not afraid nor ashamed to be identified with His Father in Heaven. He knows he is honoured by it, for His Father's name is great in all the world. He is very powerful. And some day he will inherit all that greatness, for the father's greatness and honour is imparted to the son.

When you recognize that Almighty God is your Father you are elevated to great honour, power, authority and Heavenly riches. How blind must man be then, when he prefers to believe that he is a descendent of an ape, thereby claiming a beast as his father.

THE SON CAN NEVER ACT INDEPENDENTLY OF THE FATHER

JOHN 5:19a, "*Then answered Jesus and said unto them, Verily, verily, I say unto you, The Son can do nothing of himself...*"

If there is one thing that can mess up a life, it is running ahead of God. Many times, in our enthusiasm and zeal, we get ahead of God. We "fix" things for Him, we "defend" Him, we solicit funds for Him, we hold "revivals" and organize programs for Him. We even go to war for Him. That is what happened in the Crusades. We are so busy doing things for God, that we do not have time to find out if what we are doing is God's will. Nor do we stop to ask Him for instructions as to how we should do it. We just jump right in; and sometimes we are ahead of time. And then we get into big trouble.

We need to go back to Jesus, the Pattern Son. He refused to "do His own thing." This generation was raised to the tune of "I did it my way." And we are proud of our independence and right to choose (even though it means the death of the preborn child). We defend ourselves and insist on being in control of every situation.

Jesus never acted on His own. He never spoke in defence of Himself. He never pleaded His cause. He let the people believe what they wanted to believe, even when they said he had a devil (John 7:20). When they said that He could not possibly be the Messiah, because it had been prophesied that the Messiah would be born in Bethlehem, and Jesus was from Nazareth, He never told them the facts of where He had been born (Bethlehem) and that it was only after He had returned with His parents from Egypt that He had lived in Nazareth.

Do we realize what responsibility this silence places upon us? Do we recognize that as sons of God we dare not speak without the Father's permission?

Sometimes, because we are kind and loving, we try to help people escape from their problems and trials which God is allowing them to go through that they might become pure gold. This is wrong. We need the Father's permission even for the seemingly kind deeds that we do.

The devil uses our good points as well as our bad ones. He makes us feel guilty when we refuse to help certain people whom God does not want us to help. I am not being hard-hearted. I know that this is true because I have sometimes complicated God's discipline in the lives of others by my well-intentioned interference.

The man or woman with money is often approached by people asking for financial aid. The person who requests help tells such a pathetic tale that the person with means feels guilty if he does not help. But, even if you are a millionaire, and have money to throw away, you could ruin a life by spoiling a person with giving him everything he wants.

How many times have you seen the beggar on the street, sitting at the corner, by the traffic light where the cars have to stop? In front of him is a sign that reads, "I need a job. I am willing to work. I am hungry. Please help!" Yet, it is a proven fact that the majority of them will not work if they have a job offered to them. All they want is money for alcohol or drugs, or both!

THE FATHER IS OUR EXAMPLE

JOHN 5:19b, *"What he* [the Son] *seeth the Father do...these also doeth the Son likewise."*

The Father is our perfect example. Therefore we must keep our eyes on Him. As we keep focused on Him we are *"changed into the same image from glory to glory, even as by the Spirit of the Lord"* (2 Corinthians 3:18).

The Father imparted His character, His love and compassion, His wisdom, His mercy and grace, and all His attributes into His Son. That is why Jesus could say, *"He that hath seen me hath seen the Father also."* Jesus is an exact "clone" of the Father. I know this sounds crude, but when we are limited by trying to put the things we feel and see in our spirits into mortal language, it is difficult to describe the true relationship between the Father and the Son.

For most of us to picture it, it is like seeing identical twins. It is hard to tell them apart. Some are so similar that they can even deceive their mothers. I have a friend who has an identical twin. One day I saw a picture of her and her sister. It was a photo that had been taken quite a few years earlier. I asked her, "Which one is you?"

To my amazement, she answered, "I don't know which one is myself. I can't remember any more."

That is the way I would like to be identified with Jesus, so that the Father would be able to say, "It is hard to tell them apart. She thinks like Him, she acts like Him, she loves and does the same things He does."

This was Paul's revelation also when he wrote to the Galatians. The Apostle Paul realized this truth when he said, "*...when it pleased God, who separated me from my mother's womb, and called me by his grace, to reveal his Son in me, that I might preach him among the heathen; immediately I conferred not with flesh and blood:*" (Galatians 1:15-16).

The great battle in our lives begins the moment we realize we have been destined by the Father to reveal the Christ-life through our own lives. We come under immediate attack from Satan, just like Jesus was tempted by him when He fasted for forty days in the wilderness.

God, the Father, called us from before the foundation of the earth to our life's destiny. Then, when we were conceived in our mother's wombs, He began, through the workings of the Holy Spirit in our preborn state, to fashion us so that we would be created to fit according to His plan for our lives.

The word, "separated" is *aphorizo*(873) in Greek. It means, "to separate." The Pharisees, who were the sect to which Paul belonged before his conversion, had their name from this word which meant, "to separate, separated ones." This is probably what Paul alludes to in Romans 1:1 where he introduces himself as, *"Paul, a servant of Jesus Christ, called to be an apostle, separated unto the gospel of God"* (Romans 1:1).

This intimate Father-Son relationship is a costly one, because it means we are separated from the world and unto God alone. By being cut off from fellowship with the world one often must live a lonely life. But if one substitutes that loneliness with communion and fellowship with God, that vacancy is filled with His Presence.

Those who have lived alone with God in desert places, or in foreign lands, or prisons, or even in solitary confinement, have often been able to cultivate such a vibrant relationship with the Father that He fills every moment of their lives with His Presence. This communion becomes so sweet and precious that one resents being interrupted by "outsiders" who, though they may have good intentions, draw away one's attention from the Bridegroom to the friends of the Bridegroom. The Bride of Song of Solomon pled, *"Tell me, O thou whom my soul loveth, where thou feedest, where thou makest thy flock to rest at noon: for why should I be as one that turneth aside by the flocks of thy companions?"* (Song of Solomon 1:7). The bride longed for, and desired only her dearly Beloved's companionship. When the Lord becomes the Lover of your soul you do not seek for companionship with His friends; it is your Beloved Whom you long for and desire — it is Him alone!

THE FATHER CAN ONLY REVEAL HIS SECRETS TO THE ONES HE CAN TRUST

JOHN 5:20a, *"For the Father loveth the Son, and sheweth him all things that himself doeth: and he will shew him greater works than these, that ye may marvel."*

When Abraham lived on earth he was visited one day by none other than the Lord, Himself. The Lord was accompanied by two angels. He had come to minister to Sarah by telling her that she would have a son; He also came to inspect Sodom and Gomorrah, to see if their sin was as terrible as it appeared to be from Heaven. As they were preparing to leave Abraham's tent, the Lord said to His angels, *"...Shall I hide from Abraham that thing which I do; Seeing that Abraham shall surely become a great and mighty nation, and all the nations of the earth shall be blessed in him? For I know him, that he will command his children and his household after him, and they shall keep the way of the LORD, to do justice and judgment; that the LORD may bring upon Abraham that which he hath spoken of him"* (Genesis 18:17-19).

We find here that when the ways of a man please God, and he has gained His respect, that the Lord will become his dear friend and will take him into His confidence by revealing His heart's secrets. There are not many Christians who know the secrets of God. One of the reasons is because we lack justice and true judgment. Another reason is because we cannot keep a secret. The Lord cannot reveal the hearts of men to us because we would talk about it to others and bring harm to people by the things we know about them.

If you know evil about a person, and you go about trying to destroy that person's character, because you have a personal grudge against that one, you cannot be trusted to know the secret of the Lord. You may be a powerful intercessor, and know how to bind demons and pray strong prayers, but God has to keep from your knowledge the thing you would use to destroy another one of His children.

God trusted Abraham to be able to judge justly. He also knew that Abraham would raise his children to bring honour to God. The family of God, Israel, came from the loins of Abraham through Abraham's son, Isaac.

Jesus was like Abraham. He kept the secrets of God. He knew what was in the hearts of men, but He never used that knowledge to destroy the most sinful woman, or the most treacherous and evil man.

When we can have these virtues in our lives, we will qualify as mature sons of God who the Lord will love and trust, and to whom He will reveal some of the secrets of Heaven which others do not know.

Jesus warned us that we cannot reveal these Heavenly secrets because it would be like giving pearls to the swine (the evil person who cannot understand deeper truths). This is because he does not live close enough to God to know His heart, so he will think we are living in deception and error, and therefore he will go out of his way to destroy us.

And the LORD told Abraham, "*Because the cry of Sodom and Gomorrah is great, and because their sin is very grievous; I will go down now, and see whether they have done altogether according to the cry of it, which is come unto me; and if not, I will know*" (Genesis 18:20-21).

Never reveal the evil report you may hear about one of God's children to the person who hates that one, because it will be used to injure and harm that person, and you will be responsible.

JOHN 5:20b, ***"And He*** **[the Father]** ***will show Him*** **[the Son]** ***greater works than these, that ye*** **[the unbelievers]** ***may marvel."***

The Father did not have to do miracles to convince Jesus of His power or of His Deity and Sonship. Miracles are given for these reasons: to prove that God is with you. And because they are done in Jesus' name, His authority is also affirmed. This gives Jesus honour before the people. Miracles also give the one who does them honour.

God will not do miracles through the lives of those whom He knows will not be able to bear the weight of the Glory that accompanies them. Great responsibility comes with miracles, signs and wonders. If you are a mature child of God, and God can trust you to have this power, without you losing your soul, then He will give you this honour. There are many who are not mature enough to receive this honour. They would be filled with spiritual pride.

The Father desires to show the world His Glory. And in these last days He will do greater signs and wonders than He has ever done before. He will close the Church Age with such a magnificent display of His power that all hell will be shaken — as by an earthquake — and the very throne of Satan will crumble. And then Satan will be cast into the bottomless pit.

THE SONS OF THE FATHER IMPART THE SAME SPARK OF LIFE WHICH HE DOES

JOHN 5:21, ***"For as the Father raiseth up the dead, and quickeneth them; even so the Son quickeneth whom he will."***

The Amplified Bible says, *"Just as the Father raises up the dead and gives them life — makes them live on — even so the Son also gives life to whomever He wills and is pleased to give it."*

We have heard, and used the expression, "He is the life of the party." What does that mean?

It means that a certain person is so full of life, so vivacious, that when he steps into a room he will bring an immediate positive impact on whoever is in the room. And when he leaves, it feels like the light has been switched off.

Jesus was that kind of a Person. He was the literal "Life of the party." Wherever He went, He brought the Light and Life of God with Him. That is because He always came from the Presence of God.

If we dwell in the Presence of the Father, we too will bring life wherever we go. We will bring hope and encouragement to people who are at the point of despair.

In the book of Acts we read the amazing account of how the shadow of the Apostle Peter healed the sick. Acts 5:14-16 says, *"And believers were the more added to the Lord, multitudes both of men and women. Insomuch that they brought forth the sick into the streets, and laid them on beds and couches, that at the least the shadow of Peter passing by might overshadow some of them. There came also a multitude out of the cities round about unto Jerusalem, bringing sick folks, and them which were vexed with unclean spirits: and they were healed every one."*

I believe the day will come again when the very Presence of anointed sons and daughters of God will emanate the healing glow of Jesus into the lives of others. It is told that when Smith Wigglesworth came into a department store, or entered a passenger train, people would begin to weep and repent of their sins.

The stories were also told that when Kathryn Kuhlman was ministering healing, the people often were healed without her laying hands on them. This happened as far back as the third balcony. People were healed while they were waiting outside the building for the doors to open for the service, and some were even miraculously healed while travelling to and from the meetings.

I know that this Scripture also means that Jesus will resurrect the dead out of their graves on that great Resurrection Day. But, if the Spirit of Christ dwells in us, our own lives are given abundant life — the same kind of life that Jesus had; and when that life is in us we can pass it on to others.

When God breathed the breath of life into His first created son, Adam, He imparted into his body, soul and spirit His own life and likeness. Sin has temporarily robbed us of eternal life for our bodies, but our souls and spirits still are eternal and will never die. And one day our bodies will also be resurrected — some to everlasting life, and some to shame and everlasting contempt (Daniel 12:2).

THE SONS OF THE FATHER HAVE BEEN GIVEN THE AUTHORITY TO JUDGE

JOHN 5:22, *"For the Father judgeth no man, but hath committed all judgment unto the Son;"*

The Father has handed over the Judgment Throne of God to His Son. When the final resurrection takes place, all men, great and small, rich and poor, shall stand before the Judge of All the Earth. The books will be opened, and we will realize that He is the same one whom Daniel describes in Daniel 7:9-10, and Apostle John in Revelation 1:14 and 20:11-15, the same One on whose bosom John had leaned on that last night in the Upper Room when He told us about the love of the Father.

We may think, "But what have I to do with The Judgment?" Yet the Scripture says, *"Do ye not know that the saints shall judge the world? And if the world shall be judged by you, are ye unworthy to judge the smallest matters? Know ye not that we shall judge angels? how much more things that pertain to this life?"* (1 Corinthians 6:2-3).

Not only does the true son impart life, He also has the authority to pass the sentence of judgment. But we must be very careful that we pass a righteous judgment in the spirit of love and mercy, even as Christ did, and not after the hearing of the ears, nor by personal prejudices, likes and dislikes.

Jesus tells us in John 5:23 why we have been given the authority to judge — *"That all men should honour the Son, even as they honour the Father. He that honoureth not the Son honoureth not the Father which hath sent him."*

The authority to judge has been given to the sons of the Father so that they will gain respect and honour. Everyone fears a judge.

Yet, the world has always mocked and ridiculed the Christians. The world has persecuted and dishonored those who will one day judge them. If they could only see what danger they are in because of their mistreatment of the saints, they would tremble exceedingly.

The prophet Isaiah saw that day when he said, "*No weapon that is formed against thee shall prosper; and every tongue that shall rise against thee in judgment thou shalt condemn. This is the heritage of the servants of the LORD, and their righteousness is of me, saith the LORD*" (Isaiah 54:17).

YOU WERE BORN TO DO ONLY THE WILL OF YOUR FATHER IN HEAVEN

JOHN 5:30, "*I can of mine own self do nothing: as I hear, I judge: and my judgment is just; because I seek not mine own will, but the will of the Father which hath sent me.*"

Many of us have been taught to be self-reliant, independent, and self-sufficient. We see others, who are leaders, who seem to get away with these attitudes and characteristics, and we think it is the key to success. But we and they are wrong.

Success cannot be reckoned by what appears to be success on this side of eternity. True success will only be shown from what we see has been accomplished in our lives AFTER we have finished our work on earth and go Home to our rewards.

Jesus said that He did not have the independent spirit which so many on earth seek after. Even in our youth we prided ourselves in how we did with our lives what we wanted to do. We heard our peers tell us, "You don't have to do what your parents want you to do. Don't let them boss you around!" And we have followed in their ways and become rebellious and undisciplined.

Jesus came to an undisciplined world, and the first thing He did was to make disciples out of independent, self-reliant men like Peter of Capernaum. No one ever told Peter what to do, or how to do it. He balked at Jesus' command to launch out into the deep and let the nets down for a draught, "But Master, we have toiled all night, and caught nothing!" No doubt he was thinking, "You aren't going to tell me, a professional fisherman, how to fish. You are only a rabbi. Go back to your holy scrolls!"

If we want to be like Jesus, we have to learn to take orders from Him. We have to obey His will in the slightest thing.

And we do that by being obedient to those whom the Lord has placed over us to help us, guide us, disciple us and direct our feet in the pathway of holiness.

Many cannot live a disciplined life. They join a ministry, but they take pride in how much they can get away with. Many times they can deceive their guides and leaders and pastors. But all these things are observed by "the great cloud of witnesses" who, together with the angels are taking note of man's pride and stubbornness. And they don't realize that with every rule they break they are bringing dishonour to themselves, both now, and for eternity.

If we are to follow in the footsteps of Jesus, the Pattern Son, we must stop seeking our own will, and seek, instead, the will of the One who has placed us into our positions and callings.

Be careful to never follow those who are undisciplined and rebellious. Don't let men be your example — even those whom you think are great men. For all have sinned, and come short of the Glory of God, there is none righteous. Follow Jesus Who only did the will of His Father, and was never influenced by the rebellious, self-seeking spirit of others. Let their rebellion be an example of what you DON'T WANT TO BE!

THE TRUE SONS DO NOT NEED TO PROVE THEIR PEDIGREE

JOHN 5:31, *"If I bear witness of myself, my witness is not true."*

Jesus never tried to prove, by the Old Testament Scriptures, that He was the Son of God, the promised Messiah, although He could have easily done so. He could have torn their theories to shreds by the Word of God, but He chose to let the fruits of His life bear witness of Who He was.

It is not by argument, nor by religious debate, nor even by observing a lot of religious rules and laws, that we bear witness to the world that we are the children of our Heavenly Father, but by our fruit.

Jesus said, *"If I bear witness of myself, my witness is not true."* We never need to boast, brag, nor try to prove to anyone who we are. Let our enemies think what they will about us. It is not our concern to prove to them, nor anyone else, our innocence or purity of heart and doctrine.

JOHN 5:32, *"There is another that beareth witness of me; and I know that the witness which he witnesseth of me is true."*

Although we remain silent, and refuse to try to prove our true identity, or the greatness of God that is in us, the Father will bear witness that we are His children.

As we remain silent He will show the world how much He loves and honours us by the goodness He bestows upon us.

The Father has many ways of honouring His children and promoting them before a critical, fault-finding and ridiculing world.

JOHN 5:34a, *"But I receive not testimony from man..."*

The true son of God rejects flattery. In fact these things turn him off and disgust him. He cannot bear it when people say nice things about him and praise him before others, it embarrasses him, and makes him feel like running away and hiding.

JOHN 5:36b, *"...the works which the Father hath given me to finish, the same works that I do, bear witness of me, that the Father hath sent me."*

Each one of us have been sent into the world for a Divine purpose. We have a destiny to fulfill. But it is only when we obey Him, and fulfill the Father's will for our lives, that we prove to the world our true identity — that we are children of our Heavenly Father.

There are many who claim to be Christians, but they never do the works of the Father.

When they stand before the Almighty Judge, their empty hands, will testify against them, for they have nothing to prove that they are the children of the Father.

It is very important that we fulfill God's will for our lives, because what we have done with our lives will prove our identity and relationship with God. A true son carries on His father's work, and does not seek to do his own will.

The spirit of independence can lead us away from God the Father. Beware!

JOHN 5:37-38, "*And the Father himself, which hath sent me, hath borne witness of me. Ye have neither heard his voice at any time, nor seen his shape. And ye have not his word abiding in you: for whom he hath sent, him ye believe not.*"

The Father eventually will testify on your behalf that you are His true son, and that He loves you and has sent you. You are predestinated of the Father to do His work and bring Glory to His name through your life.

You will be rejected by those who are not the Father's children. At first this will hurt and grieve you deeply, but you must understand, like your Elder Brother Jesus did, that the reason they reject you as a son of God is because they, themselves, do not truly belong to His family, though they think that they do, because men have told them they are "saved." But Jesus said they never have heard God's voice at any time, nor does His Word abide in their hearts.

The Church is full of those who really believe they are Christians, but they have never been born again and don't know God.

JOHN 5:38-40, "*And ye have not his word abiding in you: for whom he hath sent, him ye believe not. Search the scriptures; for in them ye think ye have eternal life: and they are they which testify of me. And ye will not come to me, that ye might have life.*"

Head knowledge of the Word of God is not enough. No one knew the Old Testament better than the Jewish scribes who rejected the Lord, the Author of their Scriptures. They spent hours searching the Word of God, day after day, but their religious pride blinded them spiritually so that they were unable to recognize their God when He was born among them, and lived with them in the Person of His Son.

No one is harder than the religious man, for he takes pride in his knowledge, his observance of rules and traditions, and the praises which he receives from his peers and followers.

The true son of God will recognize the sonship in his brothers and sisters, and give honour to whom honour is due.

He will have faith in every word spoken by their Elder Brother, Jesus, the Pattern Son.

And when he "searches" the Scriptures it will be an open book to him, and he shall know the depth of the Truth of God because he knows the Author, Who lives in his heart, and has given him His mind when he was born again of the Holy Spirit.

BEWARE OF SEEKING HONOUR FROM MAN

JOHN 5:41, *"I receive not honour from men."*

The true son of the Father does not let the praises and honour of other human beings, like himself, get to him. He knows what is in man, and that some of those who shouted, "*Hosanna to the Son of David!*" less than a week later were capable of screaming, *"Crucify Him! Crucify Him!"*

And is it any wonder that people can be so changeable, when even Peter, who said that he was ready to go to prison and to death before he denied that he knew the Lord, a little while later swore and cursed, and said, "I know not the man," when questioned by a maid and a servant about his relationship with Jesus! (Luke 22:33, 54-61).

We, as true children of the Father, must follow the example set for us by His Son, Jesus, and seek only for the praises of God, and long only to hear His *"Well done, thou good and faithful servant: thou hast been faithful over a few things, I will make thee ruler over many things: enter thou into the joy of thy Lord"* (Matthew 25:21).

His is the only approval we desire. We may fail the expectations of our loved ones, but we must strive to never fail the expectations of our Lord.

JOHN 5:42-43, *"But I know you, that ye have not the love of God in you. I am come in my Father's name, and ye receive me not: if another shall come in his own name, him ye will receive."*

It was their lack of love that blinded their eyes. They were not able to receive Jesus, Who is Divine Love in the person of man, because they had no love in their hearts.

If you are rejected by those whom you love, it is because love responds to love, and when the heart does not have the capacity of returning love, it is not capable of receiving love.

Love enlightens the soul of man. Without love, the soul is in darkness. That darkened soul is capable of rejecting the one who is sent by the Lord to him, even though the messenger comes with love.

The dreadful thing about that is that this same person, who rejects the Lover, will accept the evil one, even the one who comes in the spirit of the Antichrist, for Jesus said, "*If another shall come in his own name, him ye will receive.*"

JOHN 5:44, *"How can ye believe, which receive honour one of another, and seek not the honour that cometh from God only?"*

The honour that comes from another human being like yourself is worthless. In fact, it is more than worthless. It can even be dangerous for the soul if you succumb to its flattery. It can become the sting of death that will paralyze your soul, and hinder you from fulfilling your life's calling, and from giving forth the message of the Lord which you were sent to earth to give.

Moreover, Jesus said that it will hinder your faith. You will lose that simple childlike gift of believing, if you seek for the honour man can give you.

It is very difficult to have both the honour of man and the honour of God. They are often contradictory. Sometimes, and in some ways, the true honour of God is given to those who have been dishonoured, hated and persecuted by man.

The martyrs who suffered torture, and death, were terribly dishonoured by their fellowmen, but they gained and obtained the eternal honour of God. We must decide whose honour we desire, and strive to obtain it with honesty and a pure heart. Do we desire the honour of man, which is but for a lifetime, or the honour of God, which is eternal?

LEAVE ALL JUDGING IN THE HANDS OF GOD

JOHN 5:45, *"Do not think that I will accuse you to the Father: there is one that accuseth you, even Moses, in whom ye trust."*

As children of our Father in Heaven, we do not have the right nor responsibility of accusing anyone. Even Jesus did not accuse His enemies nor bring an evil report against them to the Father.

He knew that it was not necessary to "report" on them. They were doing a good enough job of reporting on themselves, and revealing the evil that was in their hearts by the way they rejected the teachings of their leader, Moses, whose followers they professed to be.

Jesus said to them, "*For had ye believed Moses, ye would have believed me: for he wrote of me*" (John 5:46). He tried to explain to them that Moses had prophesied about His coming, and if they rejected Him, they were also rejecting Moses.

They were trusting that by obeying the Laws of Moses they would receive Eternal Life. But when they rejected the One of Whom Moses spoke, they were actually rejecting Moses.

Up until the coming of Jesus the only way of salvation was by obeying the Law of Moses. When they failed in one of the many Commandments, they were guilty of failing them all, and were lost (James 2:10).

Their own conduct testified against them.

Beloved, the conduct of your enemies testifies against them. You can rest your case in the Father's hands. You don't need to do a single thing to prove your innocence nor your righteousness before the Father. He knows who are His, and who are not His.

You don't need to even pray against your enemies. Leave your accusers in the Father's hands. He is capable of judging your case, for He is watching them, hearing all that they speak, and knowing even their thoughts, plans and schemes. He will judge accordingly, and His judgment will be with equity. They will suffer much for the evil they have done, and spoken against you, because you are a child of God, and the Spirit of God dwells in you.

Even though you may not know what they have done against you, or the evil they have spoken against you, they will be judged, for they did not only come against you, they also came against the Holy Spirit who dwells in you because you are the Father's beloved child (Jeremiah 5:12).

John Chapter Six

THE SONS OF GOD HAVE BEEN SEALED BY THE HOLY SPIRIT

JOHN 6:27, *"Labour not for the meat which perisheth, but for that meat which endureth unto everlasting life, which the Son of man shall give unto you: for him hath God the Father sealed."*

The word "sealed" is *sphragizo*(4972) in Greek. It comes from the word *sphragis,* which could mean "strengthened, a signet (as protecting from misappropriation by the stamp impressed), a mark of privacy, or genuineness, to seal. It is a private mark for security or preservation, to keep secret, to attest."

The mark, the seal of security and recognition and protection is given to the Son from the Father. We, as children of God, also have the same seal. Paul says in Ephesians 1:13 *"... in whom also after that ye believed, ye were sealed with that Holy Spirit of promise."* And again in Ephesians 4:30, he writes, *"And grieve not the Holy Spirit of God, whereby ye are sealed unto the day of redemption."*

In Revelation, chapter seven, we read how 12,000 from twelve different tribes of Israel are sealed for protection in the days of The Great Tribulation.

So, we see that the Son was sealed, the children of God are sealed, and 12,000 from twelve of the tribes of Israel. Not all are sealed — only those who have the mark of the Holy Spirit in their lives.

WE HAVE BEEN BORN FOR A SPECIAL PURPOSE

JOHN 6:38, "*...I came down from heaven, not to do mine own will, but the will of him that sent me.*"

Even as Jesus left Heaven, and was born on this earth to do the Father's will, so we, who are His children also have been born of the Spirit for a Divine purpose.

It is very important that we fulfil our Divine Commission, and do the Father's will.

Yet many of God's children never stop to think what that Divine Commission for their lives might be. They make their own plans, and then ask God to bless them.

Jesus fulfilled the will of His Father in every detail. He told the people that He was the Bread that came down from Heaven. Bread is given by God that all who eat it may have life.

Jesus lived on earth so that He could be broken bread, so that people could live. We too, as children of God, must be willing to become "broken bread" that others might live eternally because of the sacrificial lives we live.

It is impossible to live a sacrificial life, a life of giving, a life of brokenness, and still live to please ourselves and do our own will.

Yet, many think they can do their own will, and still please the Father. They are missing the mark. They are far from the Father's purpose for their lives.

Some may say, "But I am pleasing God. I am doing His will, because I preach and teach God's Word."

It is possible to be in the ministry, and still be out of the will of God. It is not until we have become broken bread and died to self's ambitions, that we can honestly say that we are walking in the footsteps of Jesus.

In John 6:51 Jesus said that He gave His flesh for the life of the world. So those of God's children, who have laid down their lives in the service of God have done so that others might live. And great shall be their reward.

Many faithful servants, both men and women, have bid farewell to loved ones, and sailed to distant lands to take the Bread of Life to those who were dying in sin. These shall be counted among the honoured ones in Heaven's Hall of Fame. Thousands of them laid down their lives, and were buried in lonely fields, where they await the Resurrection Morning. Some suffered long years in cruel and dreadful internment camps — like Eric Little, the hero of *Chariots of Fire*, who died in one in China. They shall be numbered with the great army of overcomers who overcame because they loved not their lives unto the death.

John Chapter Seven

OBEDIENCE TO GOD WILL HELP TO KEEP YOU FROM ERROR

JOHN 7:16-18, *"Jesus answered them, and said, My doctrine is not mine, but his that sent me. If any man will do his will, he shall know of the doctrine, whether it be of God, or whether I speak of myself. He that speaketh of himself seeketh his own glory: but he that seeketh his glory that sent him, the same is true, and no unrighteousness is in him."*

One often wonders how Christians can go astray from the Truth and begin to follow false teachings. Error is often an overemphasis of a truth. It is a lack of scriptural balance. Scripture must be compared with Scripture. It is wrong to build a doctrine on a parable. It is also wrong to build a doctrine on one scripture. It is by the affirmation of more than one witness that a truth is established.

Here Jesus gives us another reason why people err from the truth. He says, "*If any man will do His will* [the Father's], *he shall know the doctrine, whether it be of God, or whether I speak of myself.*"

One of the prerequisites of knowing truth is a life of obedience to God. Often those who go astray are those who twist the Scripture to suit their life-style. Someone said that if you want to sin you can find a Scripture that will "agree" with your interpretation of what is right and what is wrong.

As ministers and teachers of the Gospel we must be careful that we teach the pure, unadulterated Word of God, which is uncontaminated by human interpretation.

WE MUST FINISH OUR TASK BEFORE WE RETURN HOME

JOHN 7:33, *"Then said Jesus unto them, Yet a little while am I with you, and then I go unto him that sent me."*

All who finish their earthly assignments will go home to the Father.

But we do not even want to think about going until we have finished our race. We must be careful to complete our earthly task.

Life goes quickly by, and in the sight of eternity even fourscore years will seem but a little while when compared with eternity.

So be brave, dear heart. Take courage, yet a little while, and you too will go to Him Who sent you.

John Chapter Eight

THE SONS OF GOD KNOW FROM WHENCE THEY CAME

JOHN 8:14, *"Jesus answered and said unto them, Though I bear record of myself, yet my record is true: for I know whence I came, and whither I go; but ye cannot tell whence I come, and whither I go."*

The true children of God have an inner "knowing" that they came from God. Just as all children (sons) came from the loins of their earthly father (Hebrews 7:9-10), so our spirits come from God, the Father of spirits (Hebrews 12:9).

The closer we are to God the better we understand who we are, our calling, our strength, our weakness, our origin, and the purpose of our birth.

Jesus knew He had been sent by the Father; and we also need to know that we are under appointment to accomplish certain tasks, and to play our part in the world.

We also know where we are going to spend eternity. We feel a pulling upward of our souls toward the Throne of God.

They say that the eagle always returns to his place of birth because, no matter how far he flies when migrating, he can never be content until he returns to his place of birth.

Kenneth Price, in his beautiful book on eagles, *THE EAGLE CHRISTIAN,* shares some wonderful truths about the eagle's eyes:

"Like most animals, the eaglet's eyes are not fully developed when they first hatch. They will not be able to focus for several weeks. However, there is a very unique property of the eagle's eyes which, when understood, will offer a great deal of light to the Christian.

"Inside the eagle's eyes are a series of tissues folded into pleats which are call pectens. Each pleat contains a fine network of lymph tubes. The lymph fluid in these tubes is electrolyte. That means it is affected by magnetic pull and operates as a conductor of electricity. When the eagle is young, and the eyes are not fully developed, these tubes are pliable. They are affected by the magnetic pull of the North Pole, very similar to a compass. The pectens adjust themselves to the lines of magnetic intensity from the North Pole in relation to their place of birth.

"As the eaglet matures over the next few months, these pectens become more rigid, and by the time the eaglet reaches maturity they are permanently set. As long as the eagle is away from his nesting ground there is a sense of imbalance. These pectens are acting as a built-in gyroscope for the eagle. There is a constant pressure in the eagle's eyes which causes pain, to some degree, during times of migration. However, the pain subsides as the eagle returns to his nesting ground. It is not difficult for the eagle to find his way home even from thousands of miles away because God has equipped him with an infallible sense of direction."

The words of a song I once heard long ago come to me as I write:

> Oh, the Throne Room looks the same
> As I ascend back from whence I came;
> And there's the sceptre that was mine before I left there;
> There I sat with all the sages
> I was enthroned with before the ages,
> And most of all, my Father, out of Whom I came.

There was Abraham, Isaac and Jacob,
And Sarah involved in my make-up,
And all the others who are in my family tree;
Down the corridors of eternity
God had planned my destiny.
And back to Him I can trace my pedigree.

I don't know who the author is, but he or she certainly knew from whence they came, and where their destiny was.

When we get to Heaven we will feel like the eagle who has returned to his nest, and all pain will be gone forever.

BY THE MOUTH OF TWO WITNESSES

John 8:15-17, ***"Ye judge after the flesh; I judge no man. And yet if I judge, my judgment is true: for I am not alone, but I and the Father that sent me. It is also written in your law, that the testimony of two men is true."***

Ye judge after the flesh. I judge no man.

Man's judgment is imperfect because man judges by his five senses — what he sees, what he hears, what he feels, what he smells, and what he tastes.

Only the judgment of God is perfect, because He judges by the Spirit of God. He looks into the heart. He knows the past, the breeding, the environment, the pressures, the stress, and the fears that work on a man's soul and his nerves to cause him to finally break down and do terrible and dreadful things, which he ordinarily would never do under normal circumstances. So when the Father judges He gives a righteous judgment.

Hannah, the mother of Samuel, knew this; that is why, when she prayed her prophetic, *"Magnificat,"* she said, *"...the Lord is a God of knowledge, and by Him actions are weighed"* (1 Samuel 2:3).

There are some who we expect will one day suffer great judgment, who much to our surprise will come off much lighter than we ever dreamed possible.

If we are to be like Jesus, we must learn to understand what is in the heart of man. We must ask God to help us find that guilty, accused soul in the Spirit. Except we do that we can never be good intercessors on His behalf.

Never judge anyone by the rumours you hear about him, or even the things you see. You may not be seeing what you think you are seeing.

Jesus never judged independently of the Father. He consulted with Him.

God knew that our wisdom and knowledge are limited and faulty, so He said that it was only by the testimony of two witnesses, who were in total agreement, that evidence would be accepted in the court of law (Deuteronomy 17:6). So before you judge anyone, go to the Father and consult with Him. But remember His Son always stands with the accused and not the accuser, and that is where you must stand also, if you are a son of God.

JOHN 8:18, *"I am one that bear witness of myself, and the Father that sent me beareth witness of me."*

When you are a son of God you have confidence that your Heavenly Father will bear witness to it and identify you as His child. He will never deny that you are His own.

Many fathers refuse to identify their illegitimate children. Our soldiers have sired children from Vietnam, Cambodia, Taiwan, Korea, the Philippines, Germany, and many other nations. But most of the time they refuse to identify these poor children as their own. They have returned to the United States, married their home-town girlfriend, and hidden in their hearts the fact that they have one more child than what they claim. But our loving Father is not so; He bears witness to all that we are His beloved children.

WE ARE CALLED TO PORTRAY GOD TO THE WORLD

JOHN 8:19-20, *"Then said they unto him, Where is thy Father? Jesus answered, Ye neither know me, nor my Father: if ye had known me, ye should have known my Father also. These words spake Jesus in the treasury, as he taught in the temple: and no man laid hands on him; for his hour was not yet come."*

There are millions of people who believe in God, or believe there is a God, but they do not know His Son.

It is possible to believe there is a God, and even to pray to Him, but still not know His Son. But it is impossible to know the Son, and not know His Father.

However, if you are very close to the Father, He will speak to your heart and reveal His Son to you, for like every Father, He wants you to know His Son. The Father will reveal His Son to you, and the Son will reveal His Father to you.

In this same way, when you are born again, you will not be able to keep from revealing the Father to the lost world, and the Father will reveal to the world (and all Heaven), that you are His child. You and the Father will have the same loving, intimate relationship that Jesus and His Father had.

Not everyone who is religious knows God. Religion *can* be no more than a system, a culture, a mind-set. It is possible to be very religious and very cruel and hard of heart, and also far from God.

But when you know Jesus, not just know about Him, but know Him in an intimate and loving way, you will also know the Father, because Jesus is the very expression of His Father.

Many times my heart longs to know God better. The best way to do that is to know His Son.

We, His Children, must also be so identical to the Father, and on such an intimate relationship with Him that when people know us, and are close to us, they will know the Father, and be drawn close to Him, because we are His expression of love and compassion to the world. Every good virtue that is in the Father is also in Jesus, and should be in us. Jesus is the Pattern Son and we are pattern children of the Lord.

JOHN 8:23, *"And he said unto them, Ye are from beneath; I am from above: ye are of this world; I am not of this world."*

Through the rebirth experience we have become children of God, and now we are from above. We have undergone a metamorphosis. The old life cannot cling to us, nor does it have any power over us. All connections to the past are broken. We have a new life, we belong to a new family, and have become citizens of a new Kingdom. We have a new Ruling Monarch. We have a new destiny. We have been "*delivered from the power of darkness, and...translated into the kingdom of his dear Son:*" (Colossians 1:13). We are joint-heirs with Jesus. We too are from Above! And the world will hate us, like it did Him.

JOHN 8:26-27, *"I have many things to say and to judge of you: but he that sent me is true; and I speak to the world those things which I have heard of him. They understood not that he spake to them of the Father."*

Jesus was a faithful ambassador of His Father. He had perfect confidence in His Father. He never doubted the honesty and purity of the Father. Jesus was such a part of His Father that He could say, "*I am the way, the truth, and the life: no man cometh unto the Father, but by me*" (John 14:6).

He was telling us that the only way to reach Truth was through Truth — even Himself.

Because He is the Son of God He knew many wonderful things about the Eternal. He would have revealed them to man, but He knew that men were not capable of receiving theses truths because they were not able to understand them. Religious traditions had blinded their eyes and put a veil over their understanding.

The children of God have the truth because they have been begotten by the Father of Truth. If you listen carefully you may pick up gemstones of Truth that have come directly from the Father of Truth through His children.

But your ears must be open to truth, because if they are not, you won't hear it, or worse still, having heard it, you will destroy these precious pearls, and then turn against the one who tried to give them to you; you may even attempt to rend him to pieces.

Jesus warned us, "*Give not that which is holy unto the dogs, neither cast ye your pearls before swine, lest they trample them under their feet, and turn again and rend you*" (Matthew 7:6).

In the Church there are Sons, and there are "dogs" and "swine," and you need to be wise enough to know the difference between them and the true children of God.

YOUR HOURS OF SUFFERING ARE YOUR FINEST HOURS

JOHN 8:28, *"Then said Jesus unto them, When ye have lifted up the Son of man, then shall ye know that I am he, and that I do nothing of myself; but as my Father hath taught me, I speak these things."*

Jesus always spoke of His martyrdom as His being "lifted up." It is a wonderful thing when we can recognize that suffering for God and dying for Him are the greatest hours of our life. Never is a man or woman more "lifted up" i.e. highly exalted and honoured, than in the hour of his or her suffering or dying for Christ.

During WWII when England was suffering under the heavy bombardment of Nazi Germany, Prime Minister Winston Churchill told the people "This is England's Finest Hour." As miserable as it feels, suffering is our greatest gift.

It was in Christ's death that the world witnessed that He did nothing for Himself. His whole life, including His death, had been planned by His Father.

If we can recognize that God has everything planned for our lives, and that our testings and trials and sufferings and death are what qualify us for greatness, we will more readily submit ourselves to the will of God, even though it may cost us tears and pain.

It is in the way we accept our suffering for Christ that the world can see the greatness of God in us, and that we are His true children.

GOD LOVES YOU AND IS ALWAYS WITH YOU

JOHN 8:29, *"And he that sent me is with me: the Father hath not left me alone; for I do always those things that please him."*

Because you too are God's child the Father is with you all the time. You believe that Jesus is with you because He said, *"Lo, I am with you always"* (Matthew 28:20).

And you believe that the Holy Spirit is with you because Jesus said He would send the Comforter to be with you always (John 14:26; 15:26; 16:7).

But you need to be assured and reminded that your Heavenly Father, Who loved His Only Begotten Son, loves you also, because He sent His Son to die for you, and He is with you always, just like He was with Jesus when He was on earth. When your life pleases Him He will honour you before men, like He honoured Jesus. So today, expect to feel the Father's Presence with you and you will.

JOHN 8:35, *"And the servant abideth not in the house for ever: but the Son abideth ever."*

The son is a member of the family of God forever. He grows up to become an adult who has a position of authority.

But the slave has only the authority which his master permits him to have. Even though the slave may have been in the household all of his life, and be fifty years old, whereas the son is only twenty-one, still the young son has authority over the old servant. That is because of his pedigree.

When you know your spiritual pedigree you have an authority from above.

Many fail to use their birthright. They become slaves of the slaves, servants of the servants, and soon sin rules over them. But God calls us to Truth, and Truth gives us the key to freedom, for freedom releases us to our God-given authority. That is why Jesus said, *"Ye shall know the truth, and the truth shall make you free"* (John 8:32).

THE PROOF THAT WE ARE GOD'S CHILDREN IS THAT WE HAVE LOVE ONE FOR ANOTHER

JOHN 8:42a, *"Jesus said unto them, If God were your Father, ye would love me: for I proceeded forth and came from God."*

The one great proof that you and I are children of God is LOVE. If I do not love another child of God it is evident that I myself, am not God's child.

God is LOVE. All who are born of Him have His attributes and characteristics. The Apostle John said, "*Beloved, let us love one another: for love is of God; and every one that loveth is born of God, and knoweth God. He that loveth not knoweth not God; for God is love*" (1 John 4:7-8).

Have you ever noticed how children usually have the same mannerisms and characteristics as their parents? You can usually see the father in the son, and the mother in her daughter.

This is true in the spiritual family of God also. Without knowing it, we, His children, through the Holy Spirit dwelling within, become more and more like our Heavenly Father. We find our lives, our thoughts, our deeds, our decisions, to be generated and inspired by LOVE, the one great factor that characterizes all of God's acts.

We love Jesus first, and then we love all His brothers and sisters.

YOU ARE NOT HERE BY CHOICE

JOHN 8:42b, *"...neither came I of myself, but He sent me."*

When we recognize our "family tree" we cannot take pride in the fact of who we are, because we had nothing to do with our spiritual birth — the Holy Spirit did it all through the grace of God. *"For by grace are ye saved through faith; and that not of yourselves: it is the gift of God: Not of works, lest any man should boast*" (Ephesians 2:8-9). *"And the life which I now live in the flesh I live by the faith of the Son of God, who loved me, and gave himself for me*" (Galatians 2:20b).

You were chosen before you were born. You were called before you were conceived. You were His child before you became a child of earthen vessels. You are not here by your decision, but by His willingness to send you. You are the elect of God, most precious. The Apostle Peter says concerning you, that you are the *"Elect according to the foreknowledge of God the Father, through sanctification of the Spirit, unto obedience and sprinkling of the blood of Jesus Christ"* (1 Peter 1:2a).

And the Apostle Paul commissions us to *"Put on therefore, as the elect of God, holy and beloved, bowels of mercies, kindness, humbleness of mind, meekness, longsuffering; Forbearing one another, and forgiving one another, if any man have a quarrel against any: even as Christ forgave you, so also do ye. And above all these things put on charity, which is the bond of perfectness"* (Colossians 3:12-14).

HUMILITY PROTECTS US FROM DEMONS

JOHN 8:49-50, *"Jesus answered, I have not a devil; but I honour my Father, and ye do dishonour me. And I seek not mine own glory: there is one that seeketh and judgeth."*

If we desire to honour God we begin to do so by rejecting all the platitudes, praises and honours that man attempts to bestow upon us.

Humility is one of the greatest virtues because it attributes all that we have, all that we are, and all that we ever hope to be to God alone. It seeks no honours nor praises for self.

The enemies of our Lord accused Him of having a devil. He denied it on the grounds that He sought only to do the Father's will.

The person whose motives are pure and clean is free of any kind of demonic influence.

Therefore, look for the humble man, the one who only boasts in the Lord, and takes no glory for himself, and you will find one in whom Satan can get no footing, nor over whom he can have legal rights to control.

JOHN 8:54, *"Jesus answered, If I honour myself, my honour is nothing: it is my Father that honoureth me; of whom ye say, that he is your God."*

When a person boasts about himself or hires others to promote his ministry and talents he is grieving the Holy Spirit because he is seeking his own honour. Jesus said that this kind of "purchased" honour is worth nothing. The person who has tried to impress his fellowmen with his greatness will never find his name in the honour roll of Heaven.

Brother J.L. Horton tells of a vision he had when he was taken to Heaven. He saw Smith Wigglesworth there. He said that Wigglesworth told him that when he died his work was unfinished. He had at least one more thing to do, but because he was so highly praised by people on earth, (and God will not share His Glory), he was taken home suddenly before he was through. He told Horton about a scale in Heaven. On one side of the scales are placed the praises of men that one receives and on the other side are the criticisms that one receives for righteousness sake, together with one's humility. Wigglesworth said the praises of man cut many ministries short before they finish their race. He also said that is why Jesus told us to rejoice when we are hated for the right reasons. He said persecution was the mercy of God so we could finish our race and receive a great reward. Horton was told to warn certain ones who are now in danger because of this very thing.

Smith Wigglesworth also told him that he was upset over the sale of books and sermons bearing his name. He emphasized, "All I ever was, was a normal Christian! The things I did were normal!"

Things that seem so important down here will appear so different on the other side. Let us ask God to help us to see everything from Heaven's point of view.

Jesus said to his enemies that the Father was the only one Whose honour He desired.

To seek the honour of man will bring a snare upon your life. But to seek the honour of God will give you the right perspective, and keep you in the way that you should go.

EVERY TRUE SON OF GOD IS BONDED WITH HIS HEAVENLY FATHER

JOHN 8:55, *"Yet ye have not known him; but I know him: and if I should say, I know him not, I shall be a liar like unto you: but I know him, and keep his saying."*

Jesus, the Son, knew His Father. Every true child of God knows his Heavenly Father. And the Father knows and acknowledges His children. He is not a Father who will deny His relationsip with His children. The Father and His Son have bonded together. There is love, respect, honour and unity of purpose and vision between them.

Yet this relationship is lacking between the Father in Heaven and many of His children. Why is this? It should not be that way. It is not a healthy, nor happy relationship.

Could it be because the children of the Father have not been taught to love and honour the Father? They have a relationship with the Son, and they boast of their experiences with the Holy Spirit, but their Father is an unknown personality in their lives.

Is that why they have such a difficult time doing the will of God? Jesus said, *"I know Him and keep His sayings."*

To know the Father is to love Him. To love Him is to obey Him. Man's disobedience and rebellion towards God is therefore the result of not knowing Him.

Draw nigh to God, and He will draw nigh to you. He will pour out His love for you from His great heart, and you will learn to love and obey Him. A great love grows by a close and intimate relationship. Desire it, and you shall have it.

John Chapter Ten

THE FATHER KNOWS HIS CHILDREN AND LOVES THEM

JOHN 10:15a, *"As the Father knoweth me, even so know I the Father."*

1 Corinthians 13:12 says, *"For now we see through a glass, darkly; but then face to face: now I know in part; but then shall I know even as also I am known."*

None of us can deny that we believe that God knows us better than what we know Him. He knows every detail about us. He knows our past, our present, our future, our every thought, our every dream and desire, our every longing, our strength and weakness, our good and our evil. He is our true Father. He also sees His likeness in us, and He knows what we shall yet be, and that we shall indeed be like Him in every aspect as we keep this vision in our hearts, and purify ourselves as He is pure (1 John 3:2-3).

As we progress daily into His likeness we know Him more and more, and become closer and closer to Him.

THE UNDER-SHEPHERD MUST BE WILLING TO LAY DOWN HIS LIFE FOR HIS SHEEP

JOHN 10:15b-16, *"...I lay down my life for the sheep. And other sheep I have, which are not of this fold: them also I must bring, and they shall hear my voice; and there shall be one fold, and one shepherd."*

The Son came to die for those "other" sheep. He knew that the Father had provided a way of salvation for the House of Jacob through the Old Covenant. From the days of Moses, Israel was saved by keeping the Law. Their righteous dead were sent immediately to Paradise. (*"For Moses describeth the righteousness which is of the law, That the man which doeth those things shall live by them)"* (Romans 10:5).

But the Gentiles, those "other sheep," were lost. For them there was no adoption, no glory, no covenant, no Torah by which they should live to obtain righteousness, no service to God, no promises of the prophets, no coming Messiah (Romans 9:4). And because they were outside the covenant, the Father had compassion on them and asked His Son, "Will you go down to earth, and lay down your life for them, by becoming their sacrifice — once for all?"

And Jesus said, "Lo, I come. I come to do the Father's will!" He became the fulfillment of the Law for the Household of Israel and the sacrificial Lamb of the New Covenant that would include both Jew and Gentile. He came to unite Jew and Gentile through his death. He knew that the Jews would condemn Him to death, and hand Him over to the Gentiles, who would do the dreadful deed. And while He was dying, they both would stand at His cross and mock Him together. But it is also true, that they would both find salvation at His cross, the Jewish thief, who would also be crucified with Him, and the Roman centurion, who would recognize Him as the Son of God! At the cross they would be united to be the beginning of that "one flock."

And so it is that the Father loves the Son, because He willingly laid down His life for the Father's lost children.

JOHN 10:17, *"Therefore doth my Father love me, because I lay down my life, that I might take it again."*

When we are His children, we too are willing to lay down our lives for those who are afar off, that through our sacrifice they might be forgiven and be united with the Father.

When the Father sees the sacrificial lives which His children live for His sake, His heart is moved with great love and compassion for them.

In the life of Jesus people who made great sacrifices, like the widow, who gave to God out of her poverty, and Mary of Bethany, who poured out her ointment on the body of Jesus were honoured for the sacrifices which they made. Jesus said of Mary, *"Verily I say unto you, Wheresoever this gospel shall be preached in the whole world, there shall also this, that this woman hath done, be told for a memorial of her"* (Matthew 26:13).

JOHN 10:17-18a, *"Therefore doth my Father love me, because I lay down my life, that I might take it again. No man taketh it from me, but I lay it down of myself."*

It is only by dying that we live. We must never fear the crucified life because it is in the cross that we conquer.

As we surrender our will to the Lord, He begins to live His resurrection life through us.

It is like the law of sowing and reaping. Jesus said, *"Verily, verily, I say unto you, Except a corn of wheat fall into the ground and die, it abideth alone: but if it die, it bringeth forth much fruit"* (John 12:24).

When we surrender our lives to the Lord it is like a death-to-self experience. But even as resurrection follows the natural death, so after dying to self, we experience a work of glorification in our lives, so that we are transformed into His likeness.

God uses our friends and our enemies to work the death experience in our lives, so that we can become more like Him. We should therefore, be grateful for those who cause us to suffer, for they work a good work in our eternal souls. Never hate the instrument that the Lord uses to form you into His likeness.

The Lord has called you to walk in His footsteps, and be a good shepherd over His flock. But it will cost you a great price. The shepherd has to spend much time with his sheep — often forsaking his own comforts and his own family. Like Jacob, who said to Laban, his father-in-law, "*In the day the drought consumed me, and the frost by night; and my sleep departed from mine eyes*" (Genesis 31:40).

The shepherd must suffer many things for his sheep. He cannot be weak or cowardly, prefer himself above his sheep, pursue his personal agenda or serve for compensation, status or recognition. His only motive for shepherding God's flock can be perfect love, for then he is worthy to be a shepherd under the Bishop of the souls of men (1 Peter 2:25).

JOHN 10:18a, *"No man taketh it from me, but I lay it down of myself."*

No one, not even the Father Himself, compels anyone to accept the crucified life. This way is so difficult, so high and noble, so exacting and so rewarding that it is offered only to volunteers. You can never be conscripted to hang from a cross and die. You, yourself, must offer up your life as a living sacrifice. No man can force you to do it.

You see the Lord in His agony, and you love Him so much that your soul cries out with Paul of old, *"That I may know him, and the power of his resurrection, and the fellowship of his sufferings, being made conformable unto his death; If by any means I might attain unto the resurrection of the dead*" (Philippians 3:10-11).

Only your ecstatic love for your Beloved can hold you to the cross as the nails of mockery and cynicism are driven into your hands and feet by those whom you love and blessed with every physical blessing of which you are capable. Only perfect death to self can hold you there as the sword of your "executioner" is driven into your side, pouring out your life's stream of blood. Only perfect death to self, inspired by perfect love for the Father, can give you the strength to die with the Crucified One on His Calvary.

Some years ago, as I was going through a great trial I wrote the following poem:

OH, BLESSED NAILS OF CALVARY

Oh, blessed nails of Calvary,
Secure me to the Cross of Christ
And hold me there!
Lest I should weaken in my love
And seek to flee from Thee!

Yea, let the blood in crimson red,
Pour from my wounded heart —
Pain do not spare!
And let me never cry out, Lord
That you should spare the rod.

For I would live as you have lived,
And die as you have died —
By Thy grace, Lord,
With all my life hid in the One
Who hangs on Golgotha.

THE ONE WHO LAYS DOWN HIS LIFE FOR THE LORD WILL HAVE A MORE GLORIOUS RESURRECTION

JOHN 10:18b, *"I have power to lay it down, and I have power to take it again. This commandment have I received of my Father."*

This word for "power" is *exousia*...(1849) which carries the emphasis of authority and freedom. It is the kind of authority which a potentate has.

Only those who are willing to give all have the honour and authority of receiving their sacrifice back. That was proven to Abraham when he was willing to offer up his son as a sacrifice to God.

Jesus said, *"...whosoever will save his life shall lose it: and whosoever will lose his life for my sake shall find it"* (Matthew 16:25).

Proverbs 11:24 says, "*There is that scattereth, and yet increaseth; and there is that withholdeth more than is meet, but it tendeth to poverty.*"

There is a loss that is gain and a gain that is loss. There is a time to get and a time to lose (Ecclesiastes 3:6).

Paul knew this great truth by experience, for in his letter to the Church at Philippi he wrote, *"But what things were gain to me, those I counted loss for Christ. Yea doubtless, and I count all things but loss for the excellency of the knowledge of Christ Jesus my Lord: for whom I have suffered the loss of all things, and do count them but dung, that I may win Christ, And be found in him, not having mine own righteousness, which is of the law, but that which is through the faith of Christ, the righteousness which is of God by faith: That I may know him, and the power of his resurrection, and the fellowship of his sufferings, being made conformable unto his death; If by any means I might attain unto the resurrection of the dead"* (Philippians 3:7-11).

The form of Glory you will receive on your resurrection on the morrow is being determined by the way you live today. Be careful how you live! You will not get away with anything. The recording angels are keeping a perfect record of your imperfect life. If you could see the botches you have made you would weep for your soul. The mockery and the scorn which you hide behind would be wiped off your face instantly. You would grovel in the dust and humiliation, and cry out for mercy from God, and forgiveness from those whom you have wounded and grieved, including the Holy Spirit who abides in them. For when you speak against and mock one of God's Spirit-filled little ones, you mock and blaspheme the Holy Spirit in them. Beware!

Two men were crucified with Christ: One mocked him and the other repented and asked the Lord to remember him. You can choose to mock, or you can abase yourself, cry out in repentance for mercy and forgiveness, like the thief who repented, and be forgiven.

Choose you this day which one of the two you will emulate.

Every man must, at one time or another, stand before the crucified Christ where he will either be judged or spend eternity in Paradise with his Lord.

CAN YOU SAY THAT YOUR LIFE BRINGS GLORY TO GOD?

JOHN 10:25, *"Jesus answered them, I told you, and ye believed not: the works that I do in my Father's name, they bear witness of me."*

Our lives testify for us or against us. Every act, every thought, every word we speak bears witness of who we are, and what kind of a life we are living.

When we are kind and loving we reveal the Christ in us. But when we are unkind, and deliberately hurt and offend others we reveal the "beast" in us.

The Bible calls the "beast" the antichrist. Therefore, when we submit to his mind we become the body that Satan wears to grieve the Father, the Christ, and the children of God.

We must be careful, very, very careful, that we do not give over our emotions to the "beast" for anger, mockery, jealousy, scorn, despising, ridiculing, hate, spirits of lust, abuse, and many other evils. These spirits make room for each other until our "house" has been invaded and is occupied by the most dreadful spirits of hell who will unmercifully hold our souls hostage.

What works does your life produce? Are they deeds of love, kindness, compassion, mercy, humility, gratitude, long-suffering, patience, tenderness, service to others, gentleness, obedience, and the giving of honour to whom honour is due?

Take inventory of your soul! Be honest with yourself. Don't hide behind a religious mask of pretense, because it will one day be ripped from your face, and you will be revealed for who you really are, for your works will bear witness against you.

Can you honestly say that all you are doing is in the Father's name?

Beware of your deeds and motives, lest your conduct and words be in the name of the "beast!" And, instead of "putting on Christ" you are "putting on the 'beast' (Satan)."

Search your soul! Be honest with yourself.

NO MAN CAN PLUCK US OUT OF THE FATHER'S HAND

JOHN 10:29, *"My Father, which gave them me, is greater than all; and no man is able to pluck them out of my Father's hand."*

Child of God, this is one of the most comforting and consoling Scriptures in the Bible. It reveals the eternal security of the soul of the true child of God.

Each one of us have been singled out and chosen by the Father Who gave us into the care and keeping of the Holy Spirit.

We are sheep of His pasture where we shall never want any good thing, and we rest in His fold during the night times of our soul, where we are protected from the wild and raging beasts of the night that seek to rend and devour us.

Oh what security! What comfort! What peace!

No evil one can abduct us from our Father's hand.

But we ourselves can choose to listen to the voices calling us in the night and go out to them, and thereby be lost forever from the Father's house. For our Father created us with the right to choose, and He will never remove this prerogative from us. He wants us to follow and obey Him out of love and honour, rather than out of fear and slavery to Him.

As we love and belong to the Father, we love and belong to His Son Jesus, for They are One. And as they are One — we and the Father (for we too are His sons) become more and more united, until we are hidden in His Hand!

When the enemy of your soul comes after you to harm you or destroy you, he only sees the Father's hand — the Hand that created the heavens and earth, and hung the stars in place — the Hand that performed all the great and mighty miracles — the Hand of mercy, love and power. And he trembles, for that is the Hand that cast him out of Heaven.

And you beloved, are hidden in that omnipotent hand.

WHY YOU ARE HATED

JOHN 10:32, *"Jesus answered them, Many good works have I shewed you from my Father; for which of those works do ye stone me?"*

Have you ever wondered why certain persons seem to hate you or strongly dislike you? You may have never done anything against that individual; in fact, you may have only shown love and goodness toward him, and yet, for some reason or another he has suddenly turned against you.

This has happened to me on more than one occasion. I have wept before the Lord, asking Him to show me what was the reason for such a thing to happen. I searched my heart to see if I had in any way been the cause of it.

The only answer I got back was the words of our Lord, *"They hated me without a cause"* (John 15:25b).

Why did they hate Jesus? A thousand years before He was born it was prophesied concerning Him that He would be hated, and that this hatred would come from one who had been his closest friend. Psalm 55:12-14 says, *"For it was not an enemy that reproached me; then I could have borne it: neither was it he that hated me that did magnify himself against me; then I would have hid myself from him: But it was thou, a man mine equal, my guide, and mine acquaintance.We took sweet counsel together, and walked unto the house of God in company."*

Jesus warned us that, because we were His followers, we would be hated also. He said in Mark 13:13, "*And ye shall be hated of all men for my name's sake: but he that shall endure unto the end, the same shall be saved.*"

Then He comforts us with the words, *"If the world hate you, ye know that it hated me before it hated you"* (John 15:18).

In His prayer to the Father He says, *"I have given them thy word; and the world hath hated them, because they are not of the world, even as I am not of the world"* (John 17:14).

Since it was prophesied, both concerning Jesus and us, that we would be hated, we must accept it as an honour from God that He has counted us worthy to suffer for Him because we are His children. There doesn't have to be any other reason than that. It is not what you did that made men hate you, it is who you are — a follower of Jesus Christ. If Jesus was hated because He called God His Father, why shouldn't we? That was why they took up stones and wanted to kill him. You too will have "stones" thrown at you — cruel words will be spoken and written against you, both to your face and behind your back. And you will suffer. But remember that the Psalmist said, when he was hated also by the powerful King Saul, *"He delivered me from my strong enemy, and from them which hated me: for they were too strong for me"* (Psalms 18:17).

Surely the Lord will deliver you also and out of it will come a more glorious resurrection.

"YE ARE GODS"

JOHN 10:34-36, *"Jesus answered them, Is it not written in your law, I said, Ye are gods? If he called them gods, unto whom the word of God came, and the scripture cannot be broken* [loosened, destroyed, dissolved, put off, torn]; *Say ye of him, whom the Father hath sanctified, and sent into the world, Thou blasphemest; because I said, I am the Son of God?"*

Jesus is quoting from Psalm 82:5-8 "*They know not, neither will they understand; they walk on in darkness: all the foundations of the earth are out of course. I have said, Ye are gods; and all of you are children of the most High. But ye shall die like men, and fall like one of the princes. Arise, O God, judge the earth: for thou shalt inherit all nations.*"

I believe that both Jesus and the Psalmist were quoting from a statement which the Father had probably made to Adam and Eve when He created them in His likeness, "*Ye are gods; and all of you are children of the most High. But* [if you sin] *ye shall die like men* [mortals] *and fall like one of the princes.*" (Lucifer and the angelic hosts of Heaven fell from their high estate, losing their rank, and Heavenly estate).

We know that God had warned Adam and Eve about eating the forbidden fruit because Eve repeated this warning to the serpent. "*And the woman said unto the serpent, We may eat of the fruit of the trees of the garden: But of the fruit of the tree which is in the midst of the garden, God hath said, Ye shall not eat of it, neither shall ye touch it, lest ye die*" (Genesis 3:2-3).

But when our first parents sinned it brought, not only a curse on the generations of Adam, it also caused the earth to be tilted on its axis, causing all the foundations of the earth to be shifted out of course.

When God created Adam and Eve they were as gods. They were eternal. They would never die, never become sick, never know sorrow, pain, fear, hatred, or any of the negative things that bring grief into our lives, aging us and taking our lives. They were created in the "image and likeness of God" (Genesis 1:26).

God had warned them that if they sinned they would die, i.e. their divine nature and body would become mortal.

But Jesus came to earth from Heaven, and gave His Divine Life, receiving our punishment in His human body. He thereby made it possible for us to obtain eternal life through His Eternal Blood, which He shed for Adam and Eve's sins, and the sins of all their descendants, so that we can be reinstated back into the family of God, whereby we can call God, "Abba Father," and have restored us to original likeness in which Adam and Eve were created when God said to them, "*Ye are gods; and you are children of the most High.*"

And thereby we understand what Saint Augustine meant when he said to the newly baptized converts to Christianity, "Let us rejoice and give thanks, for we have become not only Christians, but Christ...Marvel and rejoice: We have become Christ!"

He was saying that they were now new creations of God, and one with Christ. So if we are ONE WITH HIM, then we are all that He is, the Beloved of the Father.

Paul wrote to the Corinthians, who had come out of paganism only a short while before, "*For by one Spirit are we all baptized into one body, whether we be Jews or Gentiles, whether we be bond or free; and have been all made to drink into one Spirit*" (1 Corinthians 12:13). "*Now ye are the body of Christ, and members in particular*" (1 Corinthians 12:27).

To the Roman Believers he wrote, "*For as we have many members in one body, and all members have not the same office: So we, being many, are one body in Christ, and every one members one of another*" (Romans 12:4-5).

And to the Galatians Paul said, "*There is neither Jew nor Greek, there is neither bond nor free, there is neither male nor female: for ye are all one in Christ Jesus*" (Galatians 3:28).

We have been incorporated into the body of Christ through His redeeming Blood and the work of sanctification which He has wrought in our souls. Without this work of redemption and sanctification we are not fit to serve the Father or bear the responsibility and honour of being His children. Jesus Himself was sanctified, for He referred to this when he said, *"Say ye of him, whom the Father hath sanctified, and sent into the world, Thou blasphemest; because I said, I am the Son of God?"* (John 10:36).

We definitely need more teaching in the Church on this vital subject of "Sanctification." For how can the body of Christ experience this vital second work of Grace if we are not taught on it through our holy scribes and teachers? We are left in a state of uncleanness and unfitness for service, and that is why there is so much unconfessed and unrepented sin in the body of Christ, and why the devil constantly puts us to shame before the world.

THE CASE OF THE SIAMESE TWINS

JOHN 10:37-38, *"If I do not the works of my Father, believe me not. But if I do, though ye believe not me, believe the works: that ye may know, and believe, that the Father is in me, and I in him."*

Jesus was misunderstood and persecuted because of statements like this one. The Pharisees could not understand what He meant when He said the Father was in Him, and

He was in the Father. Even today men cannot understand clearly the three Persons of the Godhead. It is a mystery.

I recently saw a documentary film on Siamese twins. They were twin girls from an orphanage in Thailand who were brought to the United States with the hopes of being able to separate them. After many months of research a very excellent team of medical people (thirty in all) began the difficult task of separating them. It was necessary to do it in two operations. The first lasted four hours. After several months the second operation took place, which lasted fourteen hours.

Before the surgery, when they were one body, the stronger of the twins dominated her sister. The smaller one had to yield to every desire of the larger and seemingly healthier girl. She lost her personality as she was controlled by her sister. But after the operation she began to develop her own personality and became independent.

Jesus came out of the Father and revealed to the world His person and His personality. He lived among us for over thirty years, and then He returned to the bosom of the Father. That is how He could say, *"The Father is in Me, and I in Him."*

Today, through the New Birth and the infilling of the Holy Spirit you can say the same. The Father is in you and you are in Him. It is the reverse of what happened to the Siamese twins. They were separated, you were united into one body with Christ. His personality and His character and Person dominate your life. You live to please Him and do His will. Where He goes you go, and what He does, you do. Your own personality is melted into His, and His personality and character take control of you, making you more beautiful and loving because of it.

I heard the most amazing testimony on Trinity Broadcasting Network, in which Reba Rambo told how when she first married her husband, Doni, she was shocked to find that he was addicted to drugs. She knew he was a Christian, and loved the Lord, but he had not been able to get the victory over drugs. One day, as he was at the end of himself, Jesus came to him and said, "Doni, I am not mad at you!" Doni was so amazed, he could hardly believe it. As he cried out to the Lord for help, Jesus started walking towards him; He came closer and closer until He entered inside of Doni. When that happened it was explosive; he was mightily filled with the Holy Spirit and burst out in heavenly tongues. He was cleansed and purged of all desire for drugs, and has lived a sanctified life since then, serving the Lord together with his wife, Reba, under a gifted anointing.

This is what Paul means when he writes in Colossians 1:27 that the Lord wanted them to know that their true riches were the mystery of *"Christ in you, the hope of glory:"*

John Chapter Eleven

WHEN WE LIVE RIGHT GOD ALWAYS HEARS OUR PRAYERS

JOHN 11:41-42a, *"Then they took away the stone from the place where the dead was laid. And Jesus lifted up his eyes, and said, Father, I thank thee that thou hast heard me. And I knew that thou hearest me always."*

As Jesus stood before the tomb of Lazarus, who had been dead for several days, He knew that decomposition had already set in, but He also knew that He was the Resurrection and the Life. He had perfect faith and confidence in His relationship with the Father. He knew that there was nothing between Him and His Father.

Apostle John said, *"Beloved, if our heart condemn us not, then have we confidence toward God"* (1 John 3:21). And again he says, *"And this is the confidence that we have in him, that, if we ask any thing according to his will, he heareth us: And if we know that he hear us, whatsoever we ask, we know that we have the petitions that we desired of him"* (1 John 5:14-15).

Only the child of God, who lives in close communion and unbroken relationship with their Father, can have this confidence that they know that He hears their prayers.

So, dearly beloved, have confidence that when you are asking Him for anything that you know is His will, that your Heavenly Father is ready to receive your prayer and command Heaven's angels to minster to you and your loved one, as His Throne-Room power is put at your disposal.

John Chapter Twelve

"WHERE I AM, THERE SHALL ALSO MY SERVANT BE"

JOHN 12:26, *"If any man serve me, let him follow me; and where I am, there shall also my servant be: if any man serve me, him will my Father honour."*

"Where I am, there shall also My servant be" are words that have been impressed indelibly upon my mind. I think the Holy Spirit has branded them into my soul.

The depth of the meaning is worthy of our meditation upon them. For too long the Church has lost the calling to meditate upon the Scriptures. We discuss, deliberate, debate, exhort, argue and quote the Word, but we do not take enough time meditating upon them. We spend hours reading books about the Scriptures, listening to tapes, and we will travel many miles to hear great preachers, but we spend so little time meditating.

Jesus is saying here that wherever I am, there you will find My servant. A faithful servant sticks close to his master, anticipating his every need and desire. He will even risk his life to protect him. He has only one desire, and that is to accompany his beloved master and share with him in all his adventures, joys and sorrows. He will not follow his master from far off, but will be at his side, going out and coming in. He will share in every one of his experiences.

Jesus was sanctified. He lived a holy life. What He experienced we will also experience.

Jesus loved everyone, and laid down His life for the world. We will have this same love in our hearts and be willing to lay down our lives, even for those who do not love us.

Jesus had perfect faith. Our faith will be strong and abiding.

Jesus was obedient in all things. We will be obedient — even unto death.

Because *"Where I am, there shall also my servants be!"* And if this is true of servants, how much more is it true of friends and children of God!

MAKE YOUR CALLING AND ELECTION SURE

JOHN 12:27, *"Now is my soul troubled; and what shall I say? Father, save me from this hour: but for this cause came I unto this hour."*

Jesus not only knew where He had come from and where He was going, He also knew why He had come into the world.

Peter, in 2 Peter 1:10-11, wrote, *"Wherefore the rather, brethren, give diligence to make your calling and election sure: for if ye do these things, ye shall never fall: For so an entrance shall be ministered unto you abundantly into the everlasting kingdom of our Lord and Saviour Jesus Christ."*

Our life on earth is a kind of school or boot camp, training us and preparing us for our ministry in the Everlasting Kingdom. As we surrender to the will of God in our lives, and apply ourselves to being trained and prepared for the Higher Calling, which is our Eternal Ministry, we will make progress more quickly here on earth, and be quickly promoted to higher service after our transition from this life to our eternal life.

Have you asked the Lord to show you why you were sent here to earth? Why did He give you this opportunity to live on this planet! What were you meant to accomplish? What good work have you come to do?

When things go hard, and your soul is troubled, you need to be sure that you are in the Father's will for your life, otherwise you will seek to escape from His plan. The thing that gave Jesus the strength to face and endure the persecution and the suffering on the cross was that He knew, *"For this cause came I into the world."* Fortified with that knowledge He was able to accomplish His task triumphantly.

JOHN 12:28, *"Father, glorify thy name. Then came there a voice from heaven, saying, I have both glorified it, and will glorify it again."*

Jesus did not ask for His own name to be glorified through his life, but for His Father's. It was His Father to whom He wanted to bring honour and glorify.

If only we could all have that same attitude. The trouble is that many try harder to honour themselves than they do to honour their Heavenly Father.

The Father told His Son that He had already glorified Him through His life on earth, and that He would continue to receive honour through the life of Jesus.

All true sons who are walking in the footsteps of Jesus, and are like Him in nature will seek to honour the Father and bring eternal Glory to Him.

Are you seeking to honour the Father, or have you brought shame to Him through your life? What does the world think about God because of you? If you have brought reproach to God through your sins, repent and ask Him to help you to make amends before it is too late.

JOHN 12: 48-50, "*He that rejecteth me, and receiveth not my words, hath one that judgeth him: the word that I have spoken, the same shall judge him in the last day. For I have not spoken of myself; but the Father which sent me, he gave me a commandment, what I should say, and what I should speak. And I know that his commandment is life everlasting: whatsoever I speak therefore, even as the Father said unto me, so I speak.*"

To obey the commandments of the Lord, and do His will, is to obtain everlasting life.

Jesus didn't only obey the Father by the works He did, He also obeyed Him in every word He spoke.

John Chapter Thirteen

"GOING HOME"

JOHN 13:1, *"Now before the feast of the passover, when Jesus knew that his hour was come that he should depart out of this world unto the Father, having loved his own which were in the world, he loved them unto the end."*

John says, *"Jesus knew his hour was come that he should depart out of this world unto the Father..."*

What a wonderful way to describe death! Even the dreadful and painful death of crucifixion, which our Lord had to endure, was described in this beautiful way. If only we could speak about death in the same manner, i.e. that a certain person "departed from this world and went to the Father," how different it would make us feel about death! It would take out the sting.

We think of death, more as a departing from our loved ones. This brings pain and sorrow, hopelessness and grief, fear and dread.

Instead, we should think of it as "going home!"— going home to our Heavenly Father.

When I was a missionary in Northwest China I used to dream about the day when I would go home to my parents. I would play my accordion and sing Anton Dvorak's beautiful hymn, *"Going Home"* with tears of homesickness running down my cheeks. Such a longing to see my parents would seize hold of my heart that it was almost overwhelming.

That is the way we should get "homesick" for our Heavenly Father, and long for Heaven. It is good for us to sing the beautiful old hymns about Heaven. The modern choruses of today have lost so much of the beautiful flavour and depth of poetry when compared with the hymnody that was written by the minstrels of yesterday.

DO YOU KNOW WHERE YOU HAVE COME FROM AND WHERE YOU ARE GOING?

JOHN 13:3-5, *"Jesus knowing that the Father had given all things into his hands, and that he was come from God, and went to God; He riseth from supper, and laid aside his garments; and took a towel, and girded himself. After that he poureth water into a basin, and began to wash the disciples' feet, and to wipe them with the towel wherewith he was girded."*

When Jesus prepared to wash His disciples feet, the Scripture declares, *"Jesus knowing that the Father had given all things into his hands, and that he was come from God, and went to God; —*

He riseth from supper —
laid aside his garments —
took a towel, and girded himself —
poureth water into a basin —
began to wash the disciples' feet —
and to wipe them with the towel wherewith he was girded" (John 13:3-5).

You can afford to take a lowly position without "losing face" when you know who you are and where you are going i.e. your future promotions. The queen of England can make her own cup of tea without being afraid that she is being demoted to the position of a maid in Buckingham Palace. Some people are unwilling to do menial tasks because they are afraid people will think less of them. If you are a preacher and you have to carry your suitcase to the airport that won't make you a "porter." You still are a preacher.

Jesus knew that He had the full power and authority over all of Heaven, earth and hell, even before He died on the cross, or rose from the dead.

We too will one day reign with Jesus Christ. We know this and we expect this, but we need to know that, even as Jesus received this Divine authority before He died and rose from the dead, so we too have received the authority of the Father even now, while we are on earth. Jesus included it in the signed and sealed New Covenant the night before He was crucified when He said, *"Verily, verily, I say unto you, He that believeth on me, the works that I do shall he do also; and greater works than these shall he do; because I go unto my Father. And whatsoever ye shall ask in my name, that will I do, that the Father may be glorified in the Son"* (John 14:12-13). That is more than a promise, it is a fact! An irrevocable affirmation of position of authority signifying to us that He has given all things into our hands.

Jesus was not facing the throne; instead, He was facing torture, shame, humiliation and death. Yet He knew that in spite of all the terrible things that would happen in the coming hours HE was in control of the situation.

It's a wonderful thing when a child of God can go through great suffering and not lose his faith. Jesus knew that He could have called ten thousand angels to deliver Him from that situation, but He chose to go through the Valley of Tears because of the good that would result from it.

When you know who you are, and where you are going, you know that through God's power dwelling in you, you are in control of the situation, and every person who plays his part in it.

It's because you know that nothing can change who you are that you can afford to take the humble and lowly place, for you know that doing the work of a slave doesn't make you a slave. Your destiny is determined from the foundation of the world.

Only obey the Lord, and all will be well with your soul, and you will return from whence you came.

John Chapter Fourteen

OUR FATHER'S HOUSE

JOHN 14:2-3, *"In my Father's house are many mansions: if it were not so, I would have told you. I go to prepare a place for you. And if I go and prepare a place for you, I will come again, and receive you unto myself; that where I am, there ye may be also."*

"My Father's House!" What a beautiful way of describing Heaven! Heaven was such an unknown place under the Old Covenant! Jesus opened the way to Heaven when, through His death, He went into the world of the dead and brought the righteous who had died in the Lord out of Sheol into The Father's House.

Ever since His resurrection, Heaven has become populated with the saints who have been transferred to that world of light, beauty and peace. Jesus called it "My Father's House," and said that it had many "mansions."

The word "mansion" is *mone*...(3438) in Greek. It means "to remain, dwell, mansion, a habitation, abode."

This same word is used in John 14:23 where Jesus says, *"...If a man love me, he will keep my words: and my Father will love him, and we will come unto him, and make our abode* (mone) *with him."*

When we have the Lord Jesus in our hearts we can have a little bit of Heaven on our way to Heaven, because both Jesus and the Father come and escort us to the Mansions above, making our life on earth an outer court to our future eternal abode.

DOES THE WORLD SEE GOD IN YOU?

JOHN 14:6-7, *"Jesus saith unto him, I am the way, the truth, and the life: no man cometh unto the Father, but by me. If ye had known me, ye should have known my Father also: and from henceforth ye know him, and have seen him."*

This is a frightening statement that Jesus makes here when He says, *"No man cometh unto the Father, but by Me."* Jesus is the representative of the Father. He is the Way to the Father.

Jesus is the Door to Heaven. Yes, many seek to get into heaven by some other way. Jesus said in John 10:7-9, *"Verily, verily, I say unto you, I am the door of the sheep. All that ever came before me are thieves and robbers: but the sheep did not hear them. I am the door: by me if any man enter in, he shall be saved, and shall go in and out, and find pasture."* He also said, *"Verily, verily, I say unto you, He that entereth not by the door into the sheepfold, but climbeth up some other way, the same is a thief and a robber. But he that entereth in by the door is the shepherd of the sheep. To him the porter openeth; and the sheep hear his voice: and he calleth his own sheep by name, and leadeth them out"* (John 10:1-3).

One cannot enter into Heaven through Buddha, Mohammed, Shiva, or even Moses. Jesus is the ONLY way to the Father. All must come through His Son. If this were not the truth, what would have been the use of Jesus dying for the sins of the world? Why sacrifice your life to preach the Gospel if there are many ways to God?

Jesus is not *A Way* to Heaven; He is *THE WAY*. He alone has ALL Truth. He alone is not only the Possessor of Life, but the Giver of Life!

JOHN 14:9-11, *"Jesus saith unto him, Have I been so long time with you, and yet hast thou not known me, Philip? He that hath seen me hath seen the Father; and how sayest thou then, Shew us the Father? Believest thou not that I am in the Father, and the Father in me? The words that I speak unto you I speak not of myself: but the Father that dwelleth in me, he doeth the works. Believe me that I am in the Father, and the Father in me: or else believe me for the very works' sake."*

When Philip asked Jesus to show them the Father He seemed grieved that they did not seem to understand that the greatness of the Father was in Him.

Some of God's children may never truly learn to know the Father in this life, but if they can know the Son, they are already knowing the Father and learning to love Him.

Someone said, "We are the only Bible most men will read." We also can add, we are the only "Jesus" that some will ever see. Do we portray His image to a lost world by our love and by our deeds? Or do we turn people away from God when we say we are Christians? Some people have bumper stickers on their cars that loudly proclaim that they are Christians, and warn others of being left behind when the "rapture" takes place, but they drive with anger and rudeness. What kind of a revelation of God is that to other people on the road?

I remember a young Hindu man in the Punjab telling me, "Sister, I love Jesus, and I always read His words, but I do not want to be a Christian." When I asked him why, he said it was because the Christians were always fighting amongst themselves. This grieved my soul. I knew that he was right.

One Sunday morning I was preaching in a church in New Delhi, India. My message was on LOVE. But the words seemed to come right back and hit me in the face. I closed my sermon, feeling sad and grieved. On the way home, one of the sisters from the church told me that, while I was preaching, the elders of the church were having a fist-fight behind the church.

These things are not only true about India. You will find the same kind of Christians all over the world. Is it any wonder then, that the world still is saying, "Show us God!"

WE ARE UNDER APPOINTMENT TO CONTINUE IN HIS WORKS

JOHN 14:12, *"Verily, verily, I say unto you, He that believeth on me, the works that I do shall he do also; and greater works than these shall he do; because I go unto my Father."*

The word "works" is *ergon*...(2041) in the Greek. It means, "to work, toil, an act, deed, labour." Remember, Jesus had just finished washing His disciples feet. He was setting an example of the kind of "works" He wants us to do. If we are His followers and children of the Most High God we must be prepared to serve our fellowmen, and to humble ourself before others. So many times we think of those "works" as great and mighty miracles, signs and wonders. But I am sure that it pleases the Lord much more when He sees us doing the "works" of serving others in humility.

He told us to follow in His footsteps because He was "going to the Father." When you retire from a job, or are called Home to Glory, it is important that you delegate someone whom you feel is capable of carrying on with your work and your vision.

We are the ones appointed for the job!

EVERY TIME GOD ANSWERS OUR PRAYERS HE IS GIVING HONOUR TO HIS SON

JOHN 14:13-14, *"And whatsoever ye shall ask in my name, that will I do, that the Father may be glorified in the Son. If ye shall ask any thing in my name, I will do it."*

The Father and Son are so close that when prayer requests are made to God in the name of Jesus, the Father Himself is blessed and glorified.

When our children do well in life, it brings honour to their parents. The same is true when we pray to the Father in the name of Jesus. God is glorified through His Son because He loves and honours His beloved Son.

We must come boldly to the Lord because He delights to answer our prayers, for it gives Him the opportunity to honour His Son.

When we do well, the Father desires to honour us by answering our prayers.

Jesus said we could ask anything in His name. It is a promise that is unlimited in scope. So few make use of this right and privilege.

We forget that when God wants to honour us before the world, He answers our prayers in a way that the whole world can see that He loves us and that we are His sons.

TRUE OBEDIENCE IS INSPIRED BY LOVE

JOHN 14:15-16, *"If ye love me, keep my commandments. And I will pray the Father, and he shall give you another Comforter, that he may abide with you for ever."*

Love is the power behind obedience. Without dedicated love it is impossible to obey from the heart. One may act out obedience, but only the love-slave can go beyond the call of duty.

Jesus reveals here that the reason people cannot keep the commandments is because of their lack of love. Love is the perfect fruit of the Spirit and it inspires one to perfection in every way. Love makes you want to please the Beloved. It gives strength and joy.

Jesus promised that if we loved Him and kept His Commandments, He would ask the Father to give us the Comforter to come and abide with us.

Some seek for the Holy Spirit's infilling for years. Perhaps the reason they do not receive is because they do not love Him enough to keep His commandments and thereby qualify for this gift.

It is the Father who gives the gift of the Holy Spirit to His children, and He gives it in response to the request of His Son Who asks Him to do so because of our loving obedience to Him.

From this verse we understand that the key to all true greatness is obedience inspired by perfect love for Jesus.

THE TRINITY OF THE FATHER, THE SON AND THE CHILD OF GOD

JOHN 14:19-20, *"Yet a little while, and the world seeth me no more; but ye see me: because I live, ye shall live also. At that day ye shall know that I am in my Father, and ye in me, and I in you."*

The full revelation of the Father and the Son's relationship to each other will only be revealed "at that day" — the day when we see Jesus again — when He returns and imparts to us His resurrection life. We may feel very much alive now, but this present existence is not to be compared with that abundant life which yet awaits us. Those who have had near-death experiences have come back to tell us that the life of those who have gone on to be with the Lord is much more real than our present form of life. This life on earth will seem but a dream when we stand before the Lord and behold Him in all His resurrection Glory.

On that day we will know that Jesus is in the Father, and we are in Jesus, and He is in us. This is another Trinity, The Father, the Son and the Children of the Father. We shall experience the complete oneness that Jesus had with His Father. Oh the wonder of it all, that we also are in the Father, for if we are in Jesus and He is in the Father, then we too are in Him.

THAT AWESOME PRESENCE OF GOD

JOHN 14:21, *"He that hath my commandments, and keepeth them, he it is that loveth me: and he that loveth me shall be loved of my Father, and I will love him, and will manifest myself to him."*

Another of the wonderful results of loving the Lord is that He will love us and manifest Himself to us. Sometimes you can feel His Presence more strongly than at other times.

There are times when I can feel the Presence of the Lord so strongly that it seems like there is another person present. It is as though I stepped out of the cold and into a warm room — such a feeling of awe, reverence and sublime wonder flows into my soul that it seems as though I am caught up into a Glory Cloud. It inspires me with veneration and sacred ecstasy. I cannot say I "see" Him, but I must confess I "feel" Him. This wonderful experience can happen anytime and anywhere.

JOHN 14:23-24, *"Jesus answered and said unto him, If a man love me, he will keep my words: and my Father will love him, and we will come unto him, and make our abode with him. He that loveth me not keepeth not my sayings: and the word which ye hear is not mine, but the Father's which sent me."*

This is the third promise the Lord makes to those who love Him and keep His commandments: He says the Father will love Him, and He, together with the Father, will come and make their abode (mansion) with us. Not only will the Lord give us those brief momentary manifestations of Himself, He will move into our "mansion" and dwell with us. It will be a permanent live-in situation.

And then He warns us that if we do not love Him it would be impossible to keep His commands.

He finishes this revelation on keeping His commandments with the explanation that the Word He was teaching them came to Him from His Father.

THE HOLY SPIRIT IS OUR "SECURITY BLANKET"

JOHN 14:26, *"But the Comforter, which is the Holy Ghost, whom the Father will send in my name, he shall teach you all things, and bring all things to your remembrance, whatsoever I have said unto you."*

The wonderful name of "Comforter" is one that we do not use enough when we teach and talk about the Holy Spirit. Because of that we lose some of the truths about the Holy Spirit.

A comforter is one whom we can rely upon, trust in, snuggle up close to, feel safe with and at peace with. The Holy Spirit is our "security blanket" which accompanies us everywhere we go.

Jesus said that the Father sends this wonderful Friend to us in the name of His Son, Jesus.

The amazing thing about it is that this "Security Blanket" talks. He will teach us all truths and help us to remember everything that Jesus has taught us from His Word.

THE DIFFERENCE BETWEEN JESUS AND LUCIFER

JOHN 14:28, *"Ye have heard how I said unto you, I go away, and come again unto you. If ye loved me, ye would rejoice, because I said, I go unto the Father: for my Father is greater than I."*

Jesus wants us to rejoice because He is in the Presence of the Father, Whom He says "is greater than I."

Jesus honours His Father. He gives Him all the Glory and honour due His Name.

How different Jesus is from Lucifer who boasted, *"I will ascend into heaven, I will exalt my throne above the stars of God: I will sit also upon the mount of the congregation, in the sides of the north: I will ascend above the heights of the clouds; I will be like the most High"* (Isaiah 14:13-14).

JOHN 14:31, *"But that the world may know that I love the Father; and as the Father gave me commandment, even so I do. Arise, let us go hence."*

Jesus can't seem to emphasize too much the Loving relationship between Him and His Father. He makes His way to the Garden of Prayer continuing to share His heart with His disciples.

John Chapter Fifteen

HONOUR THE ROOT OUT OF WHICH YOU HAVE COME

JOHN 15:1, *"I am the true vine, and my Father is the husbandman."*

Jesus acknowledges the greatness and the superiority of the Father. Jesus does not claim that He is the greater. Again we see His humility and subordination to His Father.

There is nothing crueler in the whole world than to see a son who does not respect and honour his father. It seems to me that, no matter what the father has done, the son must try to find some way to honour his position, if not his person.

A country may have a despot for a king, an immoral man for a president and a tyrant dictator, but the citizens of that country must respect the office, even if they cannot respect the man, himself.

And so it is that even the most cruel and wicked father is to be honoured in some way by his children. Who knows, maybe, through perfect love he will change! Paul said he was "the chiefest of sinners." We know he was a persecutor of Christ and His children. He worked hard to destroy the Early Church. Look how God changed him! Never give up your hope in a person. It may not happen until the one for whom you are praying is on his deathbed. I have seen cases where the cruelest husbands, who have mistreated and persecuted their wives through their entire marriage, have been changed the last weeks of their lives. For when the evil spirits, who had controlled them all their lives, knew they were going to die they came out of them, leaving them with their original God-given personalities and natures, which had formerly been in submission to the demons that had controlled them for so long. The wives of some of these men have said to me, "Sister Gwen, it was the best time of our whole marriage. He was so different that last while. Why couldn't we have had a marriage like that all of our lives?"

Jesus says that the Father is the Gardener who takes care of and nourishes His vineyard. When we are in Christ, we must understand that He takes care of us also. For Jesus is the vine and we are the branches. Therefore we receive the same loving care that He does, for we bear the fruit. It is not the trunk, nor the vine that bears the fruit, it is the branches. And if we abide in Him we shall bear much fruit. But if we separate ourselves from Him, we will wither up and die (John 15:2-8).

THE FATHER IS GLORIFIED WHEN YOUR LIFE HAS MANY VIRTUES

JOHN 15:8, *"Herein is my Father glorified, that ye bear much fruit; so shall ye be my disciples."*

We glorify, bring honour and exalt the Father through our godly, Spirit-filled lives. The "fruit" that Jesus is speaking about here is not soul-winning — as wonderful as that is, but it is the attributes, the virtues, that are the true fruit of our lives. Paul named nine of them in Galatians, but there are many more. The nine which Paul named are mentioned in his letter to the Church in Galatia, *"But the fruit of the Spirit is love, joy, peace, longsuffering, gentleness, goodness, faith, Meekness, temperance:"* (Galatians 5:22-23).

In Ephesians 5:9 Paul writes, "*(For the fruit of the Spirit is in all goodness and righteousness and truth).*"

James, in speaking about the fruit of the Spirit writes, "*But the wisdom that is from above is first pure, then peaceable, gentle, and easy to be entreated, full of mercy and good fruits, without partiality, and without hypocrisy*" (James 3:17). Let us list them alphabetically:

faith
gentleness
genuineness (without hypocrisy)
goodness
impartiality (without partiality)
joy
longsuffering
love
meekness
mercy
peace
righteousness
sympathy (easily entreated)
temperance
truth

And I am sure that if we took time we could find more.

There is no age limit to being fruitful. The Psalmist said "*Those that be planted in the house of the LORD shall flourish in the courts of our God. They shall still bring forth fruit in old age; they shall be fat and flourishing*" (Psalms 92:13-14).

WE ARE ORDAINED TO CONTINUE IN HIS LOVE

JOHN 15:9, *"As the Father hath loved me, so have I loved you: continue ye in my love."*

Was there ever a love greater than the Father's love for His Beloved Son? It is great, eternal and unfailing. It is the kind of love one describes as Perfect Love.

And Jesus loved the Father with the same great, perfect love.

Now Jesus tells us that this same love should fill our hearts so that we can continue to love as He has loved. It seems like a "tall order." But it must be possible, or He would not have asked this of us.

Oh, beloved, in this world where the love of many is waxing cold and fading away, let us reach out to God and ask Him to immerse us in His love so that we can bring forth the first, and most important of all fruit of the Spirit, LOVE!

ONLY CLOSE FRIENDS SHARE SECRETS

JOHN 15:15, *"Henceforth I call you not servants; for the servant knoweth not what his lord doeth: but I have called you friends; for all things that I have heard of my Father I have made known unto you."*

Love changes our relationship with the Father. There are many kinds of love: There is the love of a mother for her child, a child for his mother, a man for his wife, a student for his teacher, a friend for a friend, a master for his servant and a servant for his master. These different kinds of love demand different kinds of responses of love in our hearts.

Now, Jesus is telling his disciples that He sees that their love for Him has become greater and stronger, so He doesn't see them as servants, but rather, as friends.

A master never shares family secrets with his servants. Friends share secrets. Jesus was sharing some of the most intimate secrets of Heaven with His disciples.

How close are you to the Lord? Are you only a servant of His, or are you a friend? Can He reveal His innermost heart to you?

We may wonder what secrets the Father shares with His Son. Here Jesus tells us plainly that He will share with us, His friends, the same secrets that the Father shares with him.

WE ARE CHOSEN TO REPRODUCE AFTER OUR OWN KIND

JOHN 15:16, *"Ye have not chosen me, but I have chosen you, and ordained you, that ye should go and bring forth fruit, and that your fruit should remain: that whatsoever ye shall ask of the Father in my name, he may give it you."*

The word "ordained" is *tithemi*...(5087) in Greek. It means "to place, to bow, to lie utterly prostrate, to commit, to purpose, to place separately, to appoint to a place, to purpose, to appoint."

Jesus is telling His "friends" that He has chosen and appointed them for the purpose of being fruitful.

Being fruitful was the first command that God gave Adam and Eve. Genesis 1:28 says, "*And God blessed them, and God said unto them: Be fruitful, and multiply, and replenish the earth,...*" We are called to reproduce after our own kind (Genesis 1:11, 12, 21, 24, 25; 6:2).

You have been ordained, set aside, to reproduce in the lives of others all that the Father has placed in you. He has already decreed and predestinated you to your particular and unique calling, and He has decreed that whatever you ask in the Father's name will be given to you. You are ordained to getting your prayers answered!

Therefore, take care of the kind of fruit which your life produces! You can impart great goodness, and you can impart terrible wickedness into the lives of others. You will have followers who will imitate you and copy your way of life. When you are like Jesus, you will reproduce others who are like Him. You can impart love, peace, joy, faith, mercy, gentleness, truth and any of the characteristics of the Holy Spirit.

IF YOU HATE ANOTHER CHRISTIAN YOU ARE HATING GOD ALSO

JOHN 15:23-24, *"He that hateth me hateth my Father also. If I had not done among them the works which none other man did, they had not had sin: but now have they both seen and hated both me and my Father."*

When you realize that people who hate you do so because they do not love the Father, it makes you search your heart about your own feelings towards others who are God's Children.

The Apostle John said in 1 John 4:20-21, "*If a man say, I love God, and hateth his brother, he is a liar: for he that loveth not his brother whom he hath seen, how can he love God whom he hath not seen? And this commandment have we from him, That he who loveth God love his brother also.*"

Love is more than an act, it is a controlling influence, an impartation, a gift from God. When we are immersed in love we become love, and give out, not only what we have, but what we are. People who have never been baptized in love are like empty vessels. They have nothing to give.

Hate is a spirit, and when one has that spirit indwelling him, it will effect his attitude without him even thinking about it, he will often find himself hating someone without a reason.

Jesus said that because they had permitted the spirit of hatred to come into their hearts toward Him, they were guilty of also hating God, Himself.

The fact that He had showed them the love of God by doing many good works among them, and that they had only hardened their hearts against Him, and hated Him even more, even wanting to kill Him, revealed their wicked hearts. He said that by rejecting His love for them they had sinned greatly, for they had rejected also the Father, because He had only done the works which His Father had commanded Him to do. By rejecting Jesus, and His works they were rejecting the Father and His works.

When people reject you and your message of Salvation through the Blood of Jesus, Divine Healing, the Baptism of the Holy Spirit, the Gifts of the Holy Spirit (such as speaking in tongues and prophecy, and casting out of demons), they are rejecting the Father, even though they may not realize it, and they are guilty of sinning against God, Himself, for this is all a part of the Gospel He has commissioned His children to preach to the ends of the earth.

THE HOLY SPIRIT IS THE SPIRIT OF TRUTH WHO REVEALS TRUTH TO US

JOHN 15:26, *"But when the Comforter is come, whom I will send unto you from the Father, even the Spirit of truth, which proceedeth from the Father, he shall testify of me."*

Here we find another name for the Holy Spirit: "The Spirit of Truth."

Pilate looked at Jesus and asked, "What is Truth?" He didn't realize that he was hearing Truth with every word that Jesus spoke. That condemned, bleeding, rejected, persecuted, hated Person with those penetrating eyes that could search out the soul of Pilate, was TRUTH.

But Pilate was blind, deaf and ignorant because he had not the Spirit of Truth in himself.

Jesus promised us that He would send the Spirit of Truth to us from His Father. It is the Father's good pleasure to give you the Spirit of Truth. He is the way back into the Garden of Eden where the Tree of the Knowledge of Good and Evil grows. As we take and eat from this tree of knowledge, we are partaking of truth. This truth becomes a part of our being, for as we digest truth spiritually it effects every atom and cell of our bodies, and testifies of Jesus to us, revealing Him to our souls and bringing us up high into Heavenly realms — until we are seated together in Heavenly places with Christ Himself.

John Chapter Sixteen

PREPARE FOR PERSECUTION

JOHN 16:3, *"And these things will they do unto you, because they have not known the Father, nor me."*

Jesus warns His friends that they will also have enemies who will hate them. He tells them that they will be put out of the synagogues (the equivalent of today's churches), and they will be killed by those who will honestly believe they are doing God's will. But that their enemies will do it all because they don't really know the One Whom they are supposedly worshipping in their synagogues or churches.

The farther one strays from God, the more he has to substitute laws and rules to make up for the lack of love that he does not have. And the more one observes laws the harder the heart becomes, until it can actually become cruel in the name of God.

WE ARE CO-HEIRS WITH CHRIST

JOHN 16:15, *"All things that the Father hath are mine: therefore said I, that he shall take of mine, and shall shew it unto you."*

The Father holds nothing back from His Son. Everything that the Father has, His love, His mercy, His grace, His power, His authority, everything you can think of, and more, also belongs to His Son.

But it doesn't end there. Jesus promised that the Father would reveal them to us, and share all these wonderful things with us. We are co-heirs with Christ in every way. Paul said to the Galatians, "*But when the fulness of the time was come, God sent forth his Son, made of a woman, made under the law, To redeem them that were under the law, that we might receive the adoption of sons. And because ye are sons, God hath sent forth the Spirit of his Son into your hearts, crying, Abba, Father. Wherefore thou art no more a servant, but a son; and if a son, then an heir of God through Christ*" (Galatians 4:4-7).

When we read these words, we kind of take them for granted, we have heard them so often, but can you imagine how they shook the world in Paul's day! The fact that we are now heirs of God through Christ is one of the most overwhelming truths of the Gospel.

Because we are co-heirs with Christ all that is His is ours —together with suffering. Paul wrote to the Romans: "*The Spirit itself beareth witness with our spirit, that we are the children of God: And if we are children, then heirs; heirs of God, and joint-heirs with Christ; if so be that we suffer with him, that we may be also glorified together*" (Romans 8:16-17).

IT WILL BE WORTH IT ALL WHEN WE SEE JESUS

JOHN 16:16-17, *"A little while, and ye shall not see me: and again, a little while, and ye shall see me, because I go to the Father. Then said some of his disciples among themselves, What is this that he saith unto us, A little while, and ye shall not see me: and again, a little while, and ye shall see me: and, Because I go to the Father?"*

Jesus was very honest and frank with His disciples. He told them clearly that He was leaving them, and they would be very sad, but He promised that they would see Him again, and they would rejoice. He likened it to the joy a mother has when she holds her newborn baby in her arms. She forgets all she went through to bring that child into the world (John 16:21).

There is a joy that is so great that it can erase all our sorrows of the past. Some people have suffered so much in this life that there is a permanent look of sadness on their faces. Even if they smile, they look like Mona Lisa.

But the Lord promises here that no matter how sad we might be because of difficult circumstances in our lives, the time will come when we will be so happy that we won't remember the pain and the tears any more. When He wipes away our tears, He will also wipe away our sad memories. This will make it easy for us to forgive the ones who have deeply wounded us.

Joy equal to our sorrow. No! Joy greater than our sorrow awaits us.

World War II was still waging when a prisoner of war exchange took place between the Allies and Japan. Some of the Canadian missionaries were released from Internment Camp in the Orient and returned home. I will never forget that first Sunday morning when the wife of Missionary Clair Scratch stood before the church and sang a special solo. She had been separated from her husband for a long time because the women and children were told to leave China, so they had come home without their husbands. Most of the time she had not known if Clair was dead or alive. Now he sat behind her on the platform of the old Stone Church in

Toronto. The church was packed. I had to stand for the entire service. There wasn't a dry eye in the audience that morning as she sang:

It will be worth it all
When we see Jesus;
Life's trials will seem so small
When we see Christ;
One glimpse of His dear face
All sorrows will erase,
So bravely run the race,
Till we see Christ.

by Esther Kerr Rusthoi

That is what it will be like when we shall see Him face-to-face.

THERE IS A PLACE IN GOD WHERE YOU DON'T NEED TO ASK HIM FOR ANYTHING

JOHN 16:23, *"And in that day ye shall ask me nothing. Verily, verily, I say unto you, Whatsoever ye shall ask the Father in my name, he will give it you."*

"And in that day ye shall ask Me nothing." What a remarkable statement! Do you realize that there is a time and a place in God where we do not have to ask Him for certain things? I think that is what Jesus was trying to teach men when He said, *"Therefore I say unto you, Take no thought for your life, what ye shall eat, or what ye shall drink; nor yet for your body, what ye shall put on. Is not the life more than meat, and the body than raiment? Behold the fowls of the air: for they sow not, neither do they reap, nor gather into barns; yet your heavenly Father feedeth them. Are ye not much better than they? Which of you by taking thought can add one cubit unto his stature? And why take ye thought for raiment? Consider the lilies of the field, how they grow; they toil not, neither do they spin: And yet I say unto you, That even Solomon in all his glory was not arrayed like one of these. Wherefore, if God so clothe the grass of the field, which to day is, and tomorrow is cast into the oven, shall he not much more clothe you, O ye of little faith? Therefore take no thought, saying, What shall we eat? or, What shall we drink? or, Wherewithal shall we be clothed? (For after all these things do the Gentiles seek:) for your heavenly Father knoweth that ye have need of all these things. But seek ye first the kingdom of God, and his righteousness; and all these things shall be added unto you. Take therefore no thought for the morrow: for the morrow shall take thought for the things of itself. Sufficient unto the day is the evil thereof"* (Matthew 6:25-34).

There is a place in God where you do not need to ask Him to meet your financial needs, beg Him to heal your body, pray for every single detail of your life. It is called "Abiding." When you abide in Him, He has promised to take care of you. He is your Husband. He will support His wife. If He doesn't, He is breaking His own law, and "worse than an infidel." Paul writing to Timothy states, *"But if any provide not for his own, and specially for those of his own house, he hath denied the faith, and is worse than an infidel"* (1 Timothy 5:8).

Surely the Lord will do better than man! Rest in Him. Praise Him for meeting your need. Stop begging and worrying and start praising and rejoicing. *"Whatsoever ye shall ask the Father in my name, He will give it you"* (John 16:23).

BE CAREFUL WITH WHOM YOU SHARE GOD'S TRUTHS

JOHN 16:25, *"These things have I spoken unto you in proverbs: but the time cometh, when I shall no more speak unto you in proverbs, but I shall shew you plainly of the Father."*

Jesus had to be careful what He said because He knew that evil men twisted His teachings and tried to incriminate Him.

It is important that when the Lord reveals Heaven's secrets to us that we are careful not to share them with those who are not able to receive them without harming themselves and us.

But now the time to be guarded about His teachings was over. The dye was cast, even then He was being betrayed by Judas. The enemy in the camp was not present. He could speak freely.

JESUS WAS MORE THAN A PREACHER OR A PROPHET

JOHN 16:26-28, *"At that day ye shall ask in my name: and I say not unto you, that I will pray the Father for you: For the Father himself loveth you, because ye have loved me, and have believed that I came out from God. I came forth from the Father, and am come into the world: again, I leave the world, and go to the Father."*

Apostle John wrote, "*Hereby know ye the Spirit of God: Every spirit that confesseth that Jesus Christ is come in the flesh is of God: And every spirit that confesseth not that Jesus Christ is come in the flesh is not of God: and this is that spirit of antichrist, whereof ye have heard that it should come; and even now already is it in the world*" (1 John 4:2-3).

When we accept the fact that Jesus came out from God, we are accepting His deity. This is the only way we can be saved. If we only believe that Jesus was a good teacher or even a good prophet we cannot be saved. We are still lost. It is only when we accept that He is Divine that we can be redeemed from our lost state.

When we make this decision of faith, we are born again of the Holy Spirit and marked as a child of God. And we are favoured with the love of God as the love of a Father.

BECAUSE OF GOD'S ETERNAL LOVE YOU ARE NEVER ALONE

JOHN 16:32, *"Behold, the hour cometh, yea, is now come, that ye shall be scattered, every man to his own, and shall leave me alone: and yet I am not alone, because the Father is with me."*

We are never alone. Not even when we are forsaken by our mother and father and all of our friends, are we truly alone. Just as the Father always was with Jesus, He is with us. When the whole world turns against you, you are not alone. Even if you have done some terrible wicked thing, and everyone in the world hates you, and all your friends have turned against you, the Father still loves you and is with you. When you are right and when you are wrong, He is with you.

The only way you and I can understand this, is that God is LOVE. And His love is unconditional, eternal love.

Even if you are cast into hell, God still loves you. The psalmist said, *"If I make my bed in hell, behold, thou art there"* (Psalms 139:8).

It is impossible to escape from the Love of God!

John Chapter Seventeen

GOD HONOURS THOSE WHO HONOUR HIM

JOHN 17:1, *"These words spake Jesus, and lifted up his eyes to heaven, and said, Father, the hour is come; glorify thy Son, that thy Son also may glorify thee."*

Glory is much like love; it is reciprocal. When we glorify and honour God, He glorifies and gives honour to us. When we glorify and give honour to ourselves, God takes His Glory and honour away from us. It is in giving that we receive. The heart that is afraid of giving never is able to receive.

Jesus knew the hour of His passion had arrived. It was a time of suffering and great agony, but He looked upon it as His finest hour, His hour of glorification.

Too often we see things the wrong way. God wants us to understand that it is when we are in the fiery furnace that the Son of God walks with us in the flame. His Presence even takes the sting out of death, for how can dying be called the *Valley of the Shadow of Death* when the Light of His Glory comes down and escorts us into His Presence!

John 17:5, *"And now, O Father, glorify thou me with thine own self with the glory which I had with thee before the world was."*

If there was anything Jesus longed for, it was to return to the Glory of God. He was a "homesick angel!" But before He could return to the Glory He had left behind, He had to experience the Glory of Suffering.

There is a certain kind of Glory that comes with persecution and suffering which is hard to describe. It is difficult to understand and explain. But I will try.

When we used to work behind the Iron Curtain in Eastern Europe we heard about a pastor who had suffered extreme persecution under the Communists. I will call him Brother John.

Brother John was involved in Bible smuggling. He didn't actually smuggle the Bibles into the country himself, but he received them from the couriers who brought them in, and distributed them to the Christians, and held secret prayer meetings in their homes. These prayer meetings were forbidden, so he was breaking the law.

Another Christian brother got jealous when he saw how the Lord was using Brother John and he reported him to the police. John was arrested and brought to the prison for interrogation. When he refused to give the interrogator the names of the Christians who were his contacts they began to torture him. They took a rubber truncheon and beat his naked body with it. They would beat him until he passed out. Then a doctor would revive him and they would continue with the beating through the night, trying to break him down so he would betray his brothers and sisters.

This happened night after night. The only one who knew about his terrible suffering was a Roman Catholic priest who shared his dark cell with him. He would spend the night on his knees every time Brother John was taken from his cell for interrogation. The priest too had suffered much, he understood what Brother John was going through. He encouraged him to be strong in the Lord.

Finally, the beatings had done so much internal damage to Brother John that he was a dying man. Because they didn't want to be blamed for his death they put him in a car, and drove to another part of the city where they threw him out of the car, onto the street, trying to make it look like an accident had happened to him.

He was found and taken to the hospital by someone who didn't know the story. He gained consciousness enough to call for his family. When they came he told them that they had to get him out of there, or he would die in the hospital. So with much difficulty they carried him out and put him on a train to travel to another part of the country. There the Christians who knew him and loved him took him, but they saw he did not have long to live. So they called a doctor.

After examination the doctor said, "There is nothing I can do, he will soon expire. Make him as comfortable as you can."

When the believers heard that, they gathered around their dying brother and began to pray that God would raise him up like He had raised up Paul when he was stoned at Lystra.

The healing power of God came down and entered our brother's body and he was healed. He was able to return home to his wife and family.

We visited him a short while after that. He still walked with a limp, but he was able to carry on whatever work the Lord called him to do.

When he told us his story, he said to us, "Those days when I was tortured were the most wonderful days of my life. The Presence of the Lord was so great in that prison that the Glory of God was upon me. Don't feel sorry for me."

We can choose to allow our suffering to make us bitter or to glorify our lives.

When the martyr Stephen was condemned to death it was recorded that *"He, being full of the Holy Ghost, looked up stedfastly into heaven, and saw the glory of God, and Jesus standing on the right hand of God, And said, Behold, I see the heavens opened, and the Son of man standing on the right hand of God"* (Acts 7:55-56).

Suffering is the gateway to the Glory of God.

THE FATHER'S NAMES DESCRIBE HIS ATTRIBUTES

JOHN 17:11, ***"And now I am no more in the world, but these are in the world, and I come to thee. Holy Father, keep through thine own name those whom thou hast given me, that they may be one, as we are."***

This is a beautiful prayer which Jesus prayed for us. He asked the Father to keep us safe for all eternity through His name. The Father has many names. Each of His names qualify His character and His office work.

When we need a *provider*, He is *Jehovah-Jireh.*

When we need *peace*, He is *Jehovah-Shalom.*

When we need *healing*, He is *Jehovah-Rapha.*

When we need *victory in warfare*, He is *Jehovah-Nissi.*

When we need *righteousness*, He is *Jehovah-Tsidkenu.*

When we need a *shepherd*, He is *Jehovah-Ra'ah.*

When we need a *Saviour*, He is *Jehovah-Yeshua.*

He is our *Keeper*, He is *Jehovah-Shamar.*
(Psalm 121:4)

JESUS PRAYED THAT WE WOULD BE ONE

JOHN 17:20-21, *"Neither pray I for these alone, but for them also which shall believe on me through their word; That they all may be one; as thou, Father, art in me, and I in thee, that they also may be one in us: that the world may believe that thou hast sent me."*

Jesus prayed for us. He prayed that we would be one, that there would be no division between us of our own generation, and between us and those first believers of the Early Church.

We are believers because of them. We have accepted Christ, and believe in Him because of their witness. They left for us their witness, and we accepted it. They wrote the New Covenant, the Gospels and the Epistles, and the Historical account of their acts and deeds, and we have accepted it all as inspired and authentic. We have even accepted John's book of prophecies, as difficult as it may be for some to understand.

I believe that the Church of today is the result of the Church of Yesterday. I also believe that the Father has answered and is continuing to answer this particular prayer prayed from the heart of Jesus to the Father.

Our oneness, our unity, our love for each other is the greatest witness that the world has that Jesus is the Son of God.

JESUS PRAYED THAT WE WOULD BEHOLD HIS GLORY

JOHN 17:24, *"Father, I will that they also, whom thou hast given me, be with me where I am; that they may behold my glory, which thou hast given me: for thou lovedst me before the foundation of the world."*

Have you ever wondered why there is this unquenchable longing in your heart to see and experience the Glory of God?

When you read this verse carefully you can know the reason. Jesus prayed that we would be with Him and behold His Glory.

Is it any wonder then, that we have this endless, aching need and desire to see the Glory? When we love the Lord we too are like "homesick angels," longing to fly back into the bosom of the Father.

IF WE DO NOT ACCOMPLISH ALL WE WANT TO, SOMEONE ELSE WILL FINISH THE JOB

JOHN 17:25, *"O righteous Father, the world hath not known thee: but I have known thee, and these have known that thou hast sent me."*

After all His years of service on earth, the mighty miracles He wrought, and the love of God He showed in healing their sick and raising their dead, He had only so few who truly believed. How sad that after all that time, Jesus had to confess, "the world hath not known Thee (the Father)" i.e. The world still didn't recognize Who He was.

He had wanted to introduce the Father to His people and show them how wonderful He was, but in the end, they still did not know, they still did not believe He was sent from God. They were still far from God, even though God had walked among them in the Person of His Son.

That was enough to make anyone feel like a failure. But it was not in vain. We, His disciples, His weak, imperfect messengers would take His message, ignited with the flames of Pentecost and spread it around the world, and in a few short years millions would believe and follow Him, even though it cost them their very lives.

John Chapter Eighteen

ACCEPT YOUR SUFFERING OUT OF THE HAND OF THE FATHER AND IT WILL GIVE YOU STRENGTH

JOHN 18:11, *"Then said Jesus unto Peter, Put up thy sword into the sheath: the cup which my Father hath given me, shall I not drink it?"*

It was right after Peter had cut off the ear of the servant of the High Priest in the Garden of Gethsemane, and Jesus had picked it up and healed it, that Jesus spoke these words to Peter.

This was the last miracle of healing that Jesus performed before His death. He healed the soldier who had come to arrest Him. Oh Perfect Love!

Jesus gave us a wonderful truth in these words: He ascribed His cup of sorrows to the Father. He said, *"The cup which My Father hath given me."*

If we can realize that our greatest tragedies have been given to us from the Lord because He found us worthy to suffer and be tested so that we can be promoted to greater Glory, we will be able to accept the cup He gives us, no matter how bitter it is.

When we had our dreadful fire in November of 1990, and lost our administration building, with all our supplies and equipment, it was a very great loss for us. The cost of what we lost was well over a million dollars — and we had no insurance. The first words that came to my mouth were, *"The Lord gave, and the Lord hath taken away; blessed be the name of the Lord"* (Job 1:21). I laid no charge against God, although I could not understand it then, and cannot understand it today. I know that God is bigger than my understanding.

But the fact that I could take my suffering and agony out of the nail-pierced hands of our Lord, made it easier for me to cope with the awful loss.

Jesus is telling Peter that the cup of sorrows which He was just beginning to drink did not come from man or devil, it came from His loving Father.

As we face the sorrows and griefs that tomorrow will bring into all of our lives, let me admonish you, that this attitude will be the key of your strength. Do not charge good with foolishness. He knows what is best! He is bigger than the devil. He is honouring us all by allowing us to "sit for exams" in the highest college of earth, the Entrance Exams For Glory! And we will pass with honours — by His grace alone.

Luke and Matthew

JESUS SPEAKS TO THE FATHER WHILE HANGING ON THE CROSS

Because of the importance of these verses I am leaving the Gospel of John and going to the Gospels According to Luke and Matthew. These are three of the statements Jesus makes from the cross in which He speaks to the Father.

JESUS COULD NOT HAVE ENDURED THE CROSS HAD HE NOT FORGIVEN THOSE WHO CRUCIFIED HIM

LUKE 23:34, *"Then said Jesus, Father, forgive them; for they know not what they do..."*

If Jesus had not begun His terrible ordeal with a heart that was willing to forgive His persecutors, the suffering He endured could have destroyed Him. It is only as we forgive those who hurt and offend us that we can continue in the perfect love of God to serve our Heavenly Father.

That is why Jesus said in the Sermon on the Mount, "*Therefore if thou bring thy gift to the altar, and there rememberest that thy brother hath ought against thee; Leave there thy gift before the altar, and go thy way; first be reconciled to thy brother, and then come and offer thy gift*" (Matthew 5:23-24).

If our hearts are full of unforgiveness and bitterness it will defile our service to God and man. We will say and do things that will bring harm into people's lives.

Even if you are not to blame for the way others treat you, it is your duty to go to them and speak to them of how you feel. Offer to clear up the problem, if possible. Many times the problem between you and that other person is an evil spirit. So by speaking in love you defeat its power to destroy you.

Jesus was the perfect sacrifice because He held no bitterness nor anger against those who crucified Him. And He cleared the way for their forgiveness by asking the Father to forgive them also, for He knew how grieved His Father was by the way the people had treated His beloved Son. So by this prayer, not only did Jesus forgive them, the Father forgave them also.

JESUS EXPERIENCED THE TORMENT OF BEING CAST OUT FROM THE PRESENCE OF GOD

MATTHEW 27:46, *"And about the ninth hour Jesus cried with a loud voice, saying, Eli, Eli, lama sabachthani? that is to say, My God, my God, why hast thou forsaken me?"*

This is one of the very few times that Jesus refers to His Father as "God." For a brief moment the Father had become His Judge as He became the Sin-bearer.

Jesus experienced what every lost soul will experience when he is banished from the Presence of God and goes out into outer darkness. He suffered that awful anguish that every soul in hell must feel as he is exiled eternally from the Lord God Almighty, and the evil spirits are in complete control over his soul, to torment him as he anguishes for thirst in the flames of hell.

That is why Jesus cried, *"I thirst!"* He felt the thirst of every lost soul, so that they need never thirst again, if they will accept Him as their Saviour.

JESUS PAID THE PRICE TO PURCHASE FOR US THE PRESENCE OF GOD

LUKE 23:46, *"And when Jesus had cried with a loud voice, he said, Father, into thy hands I commend my spirit: and having said thus, he gave up the ghost."*

These are the last recorded words that Jesus spoke to His Father before His death. Peace has settled down upon His soul. No longer does He feel forsaken by the Father. The communion has been restored. It had all been a part of the bitter cup which He had to drink.

Now He resigns His spirit into the care of the Father as He descends into Sheol to complete His great work of redemption.

We may pass through terrible dark nights of the soul, when it feels as though we are forsaken by God. But let us not despair! The Lord will return to us when He has accomplished what needs to be accomplished in our lives. Jesus paid the price to purchase for us the Presence of the Father in our lives. So do not despair, dear heart, the Lord will soon make Himself real to you again, and this terrible time of darkness and aloneness will only be a memory.

John Chapter Twenty

THE FIRST CALL TO WOMEN TO PROCLAIM THE GLAD MESSAGE OF THE RESURRECTION WAS GIVEN AS JESUS WAS ASCENDING TO THE FATHER

JOHN 20:17, *"Jesus saith unto her, Touch me not; for I am not yet ascended to my Father: but go to my brethren, and say unto them, I ascend unto my Father, and your Father; and to my God, and your God."*

We return to the Gospel of John for the final two verses.

It is the morning of His resurrection, and Jesus is speaking to Mary Magdalene.

He has just seized the keys of death and hell, and is leading the righteous dead out of Sheol to His Father's House of many mansions. In a moment He will be standing before the Father. All of Heaven is waiting for Him. The Angelic Choirs are anticipating His arrival — triumphant from the Grave, triumphant from Sheol, triumphant over death. They are waiting to receive His Blood that was shed for the sins of the world. All of Heaven is on tiptoes; in a moment the greatest Hallelujah Chorus of all time will be heard from one galaxy to another as all of God's redeemed creation and the angels, who never fell, join in together in the Anthem of Praise for which the ages have been waiting.

And suddenly, He pauses! The Lord of Glory pauses! On His way to His beloved Father, He pauses! With all the Glory that awaits to invest Him, He pauses:

He hears a woman weeping! The voice is familiar. It is Mary of Magdalene. He stops. All of Heaven has to wait until He comforts her. In the semi-darkness of the early dawn He speaks her name, "Mary."

When she realizes it is her Lord Who stands there in the Garden, she reaches out to take hold of Him. She never wants to let Him go again.

It is then He speaks these immortal words, *"Touch me not; for I am not yet ascended to my Father: but go to my brethren, and say unto them, I ascend unto my Father, and your Father; and to my God, and your God"* (John 20:17).

It isn't time to touch Him yet. Later, He will tell Thomas to put his finger in His nail-prints and his hand in His side, but right then, He is in transition.

It is in that glorious moment that He does two very important things. He reveals to her that His Father is her Father and He commissions her to tell the brethren that He is risen.

Mary becomes the first person after the resurrection to be commissioned by Christ to preach the Gospel of Resurrection.

JOHN 20:21, *"Then said Jesus to them again, Peace be unto you: as my Father hath sent me, even so send I you."*

Jesus is suddenly standing in the room with His disciples. It is the same room where He had eaten the Passover meal with them and talked with them about His Father and His Glory just three days earlier.

He will soon leave them and they will have to carry on with His ministry. Their hearts are sad, troubled and confused. Their minds are filled with questions.

He speaks, "*Shalom!*" And then He commissions them, *"As the Father hath sent me, even so send I you."* The same calling, the same vocation that He had received of the Father is now imparted to them — A vocation to live for God and one's fellowman, to serve the Lord, to love souls, to do good deeds, to preach the Gospel with the same enduement of power which He had received from the Father.

The peace of God descends upon them. Their faith is enlarged, and the vision of a world waiting to hear the Gospel message fills their hearts. It's the call of the nations. The call to take His message of love, hope, and redeeming grace to the nations of the world. For this call they will sacrifice all, and for this call, all but John laid down their lives.

For did He not say, *"As my Father hath sent me, so send I you!"*

And so we place our feet in His sandals, dusty with the sands of Galilee, and taking up our cross, we follow Him, commissioned by His Father, Who is also our Father.

CONCLUSION

The Apostle John, whose testimony we have studied, besides being the author of Revelation, also wrote three beautiful letters which are preserved in our New Testament: 1 John, 2 John and 3 John. Perhaps, of all the disciples none were more qualified to speak on this subject than John, for he was the closest to our Lord. Also, his was the Gospel the Father told me to study carefully when I was in the Throne Room.

I have often pondered over John's words in 1 John 3:2-3, *"Beloved, now are we the sons of God, and it doth not yet appear what we shall be: but we know that, when he shall appear, we shall be like him; for we shall see him as he is. And every man that hath this hope in him purifieth himself, even as he is pure."*

John was anticipating the day when we will receive back again our redeemed bodies, raised in the likeness and image of the Father. For he says, *"We shall be like Him."* This has been the longing of all who have had this revelation of truth, and kept it alive in their hearts.

When God created Adam and Eve, He created them in the image and likeness of God (Genesis 1:26).

When Adam's sons were born, they were in the likeness of Adam, who was in the likeness of God (Genesis 5:1-3).

Until Jesus came to earth, man had had very little revelation of the likeness of God. The only being that resembled God in any way, was man himself, who was made in His image and likeness, but who had been marred and scarred by sin and death.

Isaiah said, "*To whom then will ye liken God? or what likeness will ye compare unto him?*" (Isaiah 40:18).

God had forbidden His people to try to make an image of Himself because He knew that there was no way they could portray His greatness and His glory. That is why He said to Moses, "*Thou shalt not make unto thee any graven image, or any likeness of any thing that is in heaven above, or that is in the earth beneath, or that is in the water under the earth:*" (Exodus 20:4).

Although man did not know what God was like, nor could they know what man himself had been like when God created him. Still, men like David anticipated the day when they would behold His face, and be awakened from the long sleep of death, to find themselves in His likeness (Psalm 17:15).

Even Paul, who had not seen the Lord when He was on earth, said, "*For now we see through a glass, darkly; but then face to face: now I know in part; but then shall I know even as also I am known*" (1 Corinthians 13:12).

This book can only give you a brief, unsatisfactory glimpse of what awaits us: both the Glory of God and His Son, and the Glory that shall be imparted unto us when we awaken and find ourselves in His likeness.

Paul prayed for the church at Ephesus, "*That the eyes of your understanding being enlightened; that ye may know what is the hope of his calling, and what the riches of the glory of his inheritance in the saints*" (Ephesians 1:18).

It is not wrong to pray that God would show us the Glorious transformation that awaits us. It is our inheritance.

Ephesus was one of the most glorious cities of Paul's day. The Temple of Diana was one of the Seven Wonders of the World. The whole world talked about the grandeur of Ephesus, with its great stadium that was 685 feet long by 200 feet wide, its theatre that was large enough to seat 25,000 or 30,000 people, and its broad streets. But Paul, who had lived and preached there, and where he had his greatest revival, prayed that the Christians of Ephesus would see the greater Glory that awaits them.

The revelation of what is prepared for us of the Father is revealed by the light of God shining His revelation Glory in our lives. He says to the Corinthians, *"For God, who commanded the light to shine out of darkness, hath shined in our hearts, to give the light of the knowledge of the glory of God in the face of Jesus Christ. But we have this treasure in earthen vessels, that the excellency of the power may be of God, and not of us"* (2 Corinthians 4:6-7).

It is when the light of revelation enlightens our understanding that we can see the Glory of God, as it rests upon the face of our Lord, and we realize that we too have this same treasure in our earthen vessels, and one day our faces will shine like Moses' face shone when He came down from Mt. Sinai, after being in the presence of God for forty days and forty nights.

It is in His presence that we receive the Glory-transformation. That is why John says, we shall be like Him, for we shall see Him.

How can this be? It is all a part of the redemption plan. When Jesus made Himself of no reputation, and took upon Himself the form of a man, He made the legal transaction that would enable man to put away forever his mortality and be clothed upon with immortality. He became like us that we might become like Him.

And it all came about through His suffering. He entered His Glory (which He had laid aside) through His suffering, and we enter our Glory (which we lost through sin) through His suffering, and our suffering. The writer of Hebrews says in Hebrews 2:10, "*For it became him, for whom are all things, and by whom are all things, in bringing many sons unto glory, to make the captain of their salvation perfect through sufferings.*"

As I already mentioned, Paul longed so much for that state of Glory that he cried out, "*That I may know him, and the power of his resurrection, and the fellowship of his sufferings, being made conformable unto his death;*" (Philippians 3:10). He was willing to suffer the death experience that he might share in all the life experiences of his beloved Lord. Paul said in Romans 6:5, "*For if we have been planted together in the likeness of his death, we shall be also in the likeness of his resurrection.*"

Paul did not fear death. For him, it was the Pearly Gate that led to the Glory of God.

It is God's plan for us to be conformed into the image of His Son. "*For whom he did foreknow, he also did predestinate to be conformed to the image of his Son, that he might be the firstborn among many brethren*" (Romans 8:29). We have been predestinated to be restored to our original pre-fall state that we originally were meant to have. Nothing can stop God now from fulfilling His plan. We will come the full circle.

That is why our spirits groan within us, as Paul said in Romans 8:23, "*And not only they, but ourselves also, which have the firstfruits of the Spirit, even we ourselves groan within ourselves, waiting for the adoption, to wit, the redemption of our body.*" We have the firstfruits of the Spirit. There already is something different about us since we were born again. We are not the persons we were before we were saved. We have become new Creatures in Christ Jesus.

But this is only the beginning. Our spirits groan for our total body-redemption — no more pain, no more weakness, no more aging. We won't need dental work, glasses, pills, hair-colouring, cosmetics, face-lifts, corsets, hours of exercise (that too is part of the curse), and many other things that we do to try to look younger and healthier. The only "pill" we will need is an "apple" from the Tree of Life.

And we won't have to wait a long time. Already we are anticipating that glorious morning as we see the rosy tint in the eastern sky that calls us to, "*Arise, shine; for thy light is come, and the glory of the LORD is risen upon thee. For, behold, the darkness shall cover the earth, and gross darkness the people: but the LORD shall arise upon thee, and his glory shall be seen upon thee. And the Gentiles shall come to thy light, and kings to the brightness of thy rising*" (Isaiah 60:1-3).

We are a chosen generation, a royal priesthood, an holy nation, a peculiar people; that are *destined* to show forth the praises of Him who has called us out of darkness into His marvelous light (1 Peter 2:9).

Our future is brighter than our past. Let us be encouraged — even in the midst of this present darkness that is covering the earth. Know this, that the darker it gets, the greater will be His Glory upon us and in us, transforming us moment by moment into His image and likeness.

—-THE END—-

SCRIPTURES

WE SHALL BE LIKE HIM

1 JOHN 3:2-3, "Beloved, now are we the sons of God, and it doth not yet appear what we shall be: but we know that, when he shall appear, we shall be like him; for we shall see him as he is. And every man that hath this hope in him purifieth himself, even as he is pure."

WE WERE MADE IN THE IMAGE OF GOD

GENESIS 1:26, And God said: "Let us make man in our image, after our likeness: and let them have dominion over the fish of the sea, and over the fowl of the air, and over the cattle, and over all the earth, and over every creeping thing that creepeth upon the earth."

GENESIS 5:1-3, "This is the book of the generations of Adam. In the day that God created man, in the likeness of God made he him; Male and female created he them; and blessed them, and called their name Adam, in the day when they were created. And Adam lived an hundred and thirty years, and begat a son in his own likeness, after his image; and called his name Seth."

EXODUS 20:4, "Thou shalt not make unto thee any graven image, or any likeness of any thing that is in heaven above, or that is in the earth beneath, or that is in the water under the earth."

ISAIAH 40:18, "To whom then will ye liken God? or what likeness will ye compare unto him?"

THE PSALMIST HAD THIS HOPE THAT HE WOULD ONE DAY BE LIKE GOD

PSALM 17:15, "As for me, I will behold thy face in righteousness: I shall be satisfied, when I awake, with thy likeness."

NOW WE ONLY KNOW IN PART

1 CORINTHIANS 13:12, "For now we see through a glass, darkly; but then face to face: now I know in part; but then shall I know even as also I am known."

PAUL PRAYED FOR OUR ENLIGHTENMENT

EPHESIANS 1:18, "The eyes of your understanding being enlightened; that ye may know what is the hope of his calling, and what the riches of the glory of his inheritance in the saints."

GOD HAS COMMANDED THE LIGHT TO GIVE US KNOWLEDGE

2 CORINTHIANS 4:6-7, "For God, who commanded the light to shine out of darkness, hath shined in our hearts, to give the light of the knowledge of the glory of God in the face of Jesus Christ. But we have this treasure in earthen vessels, that the excellency of the power may be of God, and not of us."

WE HAVE BECOME A "NEW MAN"

COLOSSIANS 3:10, "And have put on the new man, which is renewed in knowledge after the image of him that created him. "

JESUS BECAME MAN THAT WE MIGHT BECOME LIKE HIM

PHILIPPIANS 2:7, "But made himself of no reputation, and took upon him the form of a servant, and was made in the likeness of men. "

HE IS BRINGING MANY SONS INTO GLORY THROUGH SUFFERING

HEBREWS 2:10, "For it became him, for whom are all things, and by whom are all things, in bringing many sons unto glory, to make the Captain of their salvation perfect through sufferings."

ROMANS 6:5, "For if we have been planted together in the likeness of his death, we shall be also in the likeness of his resurrection."

PHILIPPIANS 3:10, "That I may know him, and the power of his resurrection, and the fellowship of his sufferings, being made conformable unto his death."

WE HAVE BEEN PREDESTINED TO BE IN THE IMAGE OF GOD'S SON

ROMANS 8:29, "For whom he did foreknow, he also did predestinate to be conformed to the image of his Son, that he might be the firstborn among many brethren."

THE SPIRIT WITHIN US GROANS FOR OUR FULL REDEMPTION

ROMANS 8:23, "And not only they, but ourselves also, which have the firstfruits of the Spirit, even we ourselves groan within ourselves, waiting for the adoption, to wit, the redemption of our body."

THERE WILL BE A DIFFERENCE IN OUR RESURRECTION

1 CORINTHIANS 15:40-43, "There are also celestial bodies, and bodies terrestrial: but the glory of the celestial is one, and the glory of the terrestrial is another. There is one glory of the sun, and another glory of the moon, and another glory of the stars: for one star differeth from another star in glory. So also is the resurrection of the dead. It is sown in corruption; it is raised in incorruption: It is sown in dishonour; it is raised in glory: it is sown in weakness; it is raised in power." ALSO VERSES 49-52.

WE ARE A CHOSEN GENERATION

1 PETER 2:9, "But ye are a chosen generation, a royal priesthood, an holy nation, a peculiar people; that ye should shew forth the praises of him who hath called you out of darkness into his marvelous light."

THE GLORY OF GOD IS ARISEN UPON US

ISAIAH 60:1-3, "Arise, shine; for thy light is come, and the glory of the LORD is risen upon thee. For, behold, the darkness shall cover the earth, and gross darkness the people: but the LORD shall arise upon thee, and his glory shall be seen upon thee. And the Gentiles shall come to thy light, and kings to the brightness of thy rising."

More Life-Changing Books

Gwen Shaw's Autobiography

UNCONDITIONAL SURRENDER. The life story of Gwen R. Shaw, lovingly known as "Sister Gwen" to thousands of people in over one hundred nations. You will laugh and cry with her as you feel the heartbeat of a great woman of God who has given all to Him, asking only for souls in return. Your life will be challenged as you walk with her through mission field after mission field. You will never be the same when you read how God pours out His Spirit and confirms His Word. Paperback................................#000102 $14.00

DVD NTSC (North American format).....................#DGSN $15.00

DVD PAL (European format)....................................#DGSP $15.00

Daily Devotionals by Gwen Shaw

DAILY PREPARATIONS FOR PERFECTION — This daily devotional comes to you exactly as the Holy Spirit spoke to the author's heart in her own private devotions. You will feel that Jesus is speaking to you every time you open it. It is loved by all. You'll read it and re-read it..Paperback #000202 $12.50

DAY BY DAY— This daily devotional book based on the Psalms will give you an inspiring word directly from the Throne Room each day to fill your heart with praise to God. Starting each day with praise is the secret of a joy-filled life.................Softcover #000204 $11.95

....Hardcover #000203 $18.50

Also available in French ....Hardcover #000203FR $18.50

FROM THE HEART OF JESUS — This devotional book will take you back to Bible days and you will walk and talk with Jesus and His disciples as he ministered to the people, as He suffered and died and as He rose again from the dead. These words from the heart of Jesus will go straight to your heart, bringing comfort, peace, encouragement and hope! 923 pages ....Hardcover #000207 $29.95

GEMS OF WISDOM — ***A daily devotional based on the book of Proverbs.*** In the Proverbs you will find instruction for upright living, honesty, justice and wisdom. Every word in the Proverbs applies to today's problems as when they were first written. If you are going through great difficulties and facing problems which seem to have no solution, you will find the answer in these Proverbs. You'll have a Proverb and an inspired writing about it for each day of the year! A great gift idea for graduates and newlyweds!......... Hardcover #000209 $25.95

IN THE BEGINNING — *A daily devotional based on the book of Genesis.* The Book of Genesis is perhaps the most important book in the Old Testament. It is the foundation stone of all knowledge and wisdom. Deep and wonderful truths hidden in the pages of Genesis are revealed in this devotional book. You'll be amazed at the soul-stirring writings inspired by the well-known stories of Genesis. Hardcover .... #000211 $27.95

DEEPEN YOUR WALK WITH GOD WITH CLASSIC ANOINTED BIBLE STUDIES BY GWEN SHAW!

BEHOLD THE BRIDEGROOM COMETH! A Bible study on the soon return of Jesus Christ. With so many false teachings these days, it is important that we realize how imminent the rapture of the saints of God really is... #000304 $6.50

ENDUED WITH LIGHT TO REIGN FOREVER. This deeply profound Bible study reveals the characteristics of the eternal, supernatural, creative light of God as found in His Word. The "Father of Lights," created man in His image. He longs for man to step out of darkness and into His light.. #000306 $5.00

GOD'S END-TIME BATTLE-PLAN. This study on spiritual warfare gives you the biblical weapons for spiritual warfare such as victory through dancing, shouting, praising, uplifted hands, marching, etc. It has been a great help to many who have been bound by tradition. .... #000305 $8.00

IT'S TIME FOR REVIVAL. A Bible study on revival that not only gives scriptural promises of the end-time revival, but also presents the stories of revivals in the past and the revivalists whom God used. It will stir your heart and encourage you to believe for great revival! .... #000311 $7.75

OUR MINISTERING ANGELS. A scriptural Bible study on the topic of angels. Angels will be playing a more and more prominent part in these last days. We need to understand about them and their ministry. Read exciting accounts of angelic help......... #000308 $8.00

POUR OUT YOUR HEART. A wonderful Bible study on travailing prayer. The hour has come to intercede before the throne of God. The call to intercession is for everyone, and we must carry the Lord's burden and weep for the lost so that the harvest can be brought in quickly .... #000301 $5.00

REDEEMING THE LAND. A Bible study on spiritual warfare. This important teaching will help you know your authority through the Blood of Jesus to dislodge evil spirits, break the curse, and restore God's blessing upon the land .... #000309 $9.50

THE FINE LINE. This Bible study clearly magnifies the "fine line" of difference between the soul realm and the spirit realm. Both are intangible and therefore cannot be discerned with the five senses, but must be discerned by the Holy Spirit and the Word of God. A must for the deeper Christian .... #000307 $6.00

THE POWER OF THE PRECIOUS BLOOD. A Bible study on the Blood of Jesus. The author shares how it was revealed to her how much Satan fears Jesus' Blood. This Bible study will help you overcome and destroy the works of Satan in your life and the lives of loved ones! .... #000303 $5.00

THE POWER OF PRAISE. When God created the heavens and the earth, He was surrounded by praise. Miracles happen when holy people praise a Holy God! Praise is the language of creation. If prayer can move the hand of God, how much more praise can move Him! .... #000312 $5.00

YE SHALL RECEIVE POWER FROM ON HIGH. This is a much needed foundational teaching on the Baptism of the Holy Spirit. It will enable you to teach this subject, as well as to understand these truths more fully yourself.. #000310 $5.00

YOUR APPOINTMENT WITH GOD. A Bible study on fasting. Fasting is one of the most neglected sources of power over bondages of Satan that God has given the Church. The author's experiences shared in this Bible study will change your life........... #000302 $5.00

In-Depth Bible Studies for the Serious Student of God's Word

FORGIVE AND RECEIVE. This Bible Study is a lesson to the church on the much-needed truths of forgiveness and restoration. The epistle to Philemon came from the heart of Paul who had experienced great forgiveness .... #000406 $7.00

GRACE ALONE. This study teaches the reader to gain freedom in the finished work of the Cross by forsaking works (which cannot add to salvation) and live by ***Grace Alone*** .... #000402 $13.00

MYSTERY REVEALED. Search the depths of God's riches in one of Paul's most profound epistles, "to the praise of His glory!" Learn the "mystery" of the united Body of Christ as revealed in the book of Ephesians .... #000403 $15.00

OUR GLORIOUS HEAD. This book teaches vital truths for today, assisting the reader in discerning false teachings, when the philosophies of men are being promoted as being the truths of God. Jesus Christ is the Head of His Body! .... #000404 $9.00

THE CATCHING AWAY! This is a very timely Bible study because Jesus is coming soon! The book of 1 Thessalonians explains God's revelation to Paul on the rapture of the saints. 2 Thessalonians reveals what will happen after the rapture when the antichrist takes over.. #000407 $13.00

THE LOVE LETTER. This expository study of the letter to the first church of Europe will give the reader an understanding of Paul's great love for the church that was born out of his suffering. .... #000405 $9.00

Popular Bible Course

THE TRIBES OF ISRAEL. This popular and well-loved study on the thirteen tribes of Israel will show you your place in the spiritual tribes in these last days. Understand yourself and others better through the study of this Bible Course! .... #000501 $45.00 • 13 CD set - #CTGS1 $50.00

THE WOMEN OF THE BIBLE SERIES BY GWEN SHAW,
opens a window into the lives of the women of the Bible in the style of historical novels. Their joys and heartaches were the same as ours today.

EVE—MOTHER OF US ALL. Read the life story of the first woman. Discover the secrets of one of the most neglected and misunderstood stories in history .... #000801 $4.50

SARAH—PRINCESS OF ALL MANKIND. She was beautiful — and barren. Feel the heartbeat and struggles of this woman who left so great an impact on us all .... #000802 $4.50

REBEKAH—THE BRIDE. The destiny of the world was determined when she said three simple words, "I will go!" Enjoy this touching story. .... #000803 $4.50

LEAH AND RACHEL—THE TWIN WIVES OF JACOB. You will feel their dreams, their pains, their jealousies and their love for one man. .... #000804 $4.50

MIRIAM—THE PROPHETESS. Miriam was the first female to lead worship, the first woman to whom the Lord gave the title "Leader of God's people." .... #000805 $7.50

DEBORAH AND JAEL. May God's "warrior women" now arise to take their place in the end-time battle for the harvest! .... #000806 $4.50

OTHER BOOKS BY GWEN SHAW

GOING HOME. This book is a treasure which answers so many questions and comforts so many hearts. It gives strength and faith, and helps one to cope with the pain of the loss of a loved one. This book is not really a book about dying, but about Going Home to our Eternal Abode with our loving Heavenly Father .... #000607 $8.00

LOVE, THE LAW OF THE ANGELS. This is undoubtedly the greatest of Gwen Shaw's writings. It carries a message of healing and life in a sad and fallen civilization. Love heals the broken-hearted and sets disarray in order. You will never be the same after reading this beautiful book about love .... #000601 $10.00

SONG OF LOVE. She was a heart-broken missionary, far from home. She cried out to God for help. He spoke, "Turn to the Song of Solomon and read!" As she turned in obedience, the Lord took her into the "Throne Room" of Heaven and taught her about the love of Christ for His Bride. Fall in love with Jesus afresh .... #000401 $7.50

THE FALSE FAST. From the pen of Gwen Shaw, author of *Your Appointment With God* (a Bible Study on fasting), comes an exposé on the False Fast. It will help you to examine your motives for fasting, and make your foundations sure, so that your fast will be a potent tool in the hands of God .... #000602 $2.50

THE LIGHT WILL COME FROM RUSSIA. Mother Barbara, Abbess of the Mount of Olives in Jerusalem shares prophecies concerning the nations of the world given by a holy bishop of the Kremlin, just prior to the Russian Revolution. Includes a fascinating history of the final days of the royal family .... #000606 $5.50

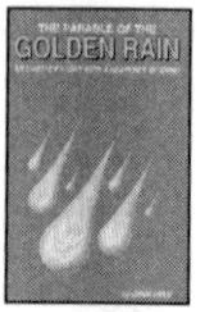

THE PARABLE OF THE GOLDEN RAIN. This is the story of how revivals come and go, and a true picture, in parable language, of how the Church tries to replace the genuine move of the Spirit with man-made programs and tactics. It's amusing and convicting at the same time.. #000603 $4.00

THEY SHALL MOUNT UP WITH WINGS AS EAGLES. Though you may feel old or tired, if you wait on the Lord, you shall mount up on wings as eagles! Let this book encourage you to stretch your wings and fulfill your destiny — no matter what your age! .... #000604 $6.95

TO BE LIKE JESUS. Based on her Throne Room experience in 1971, the author shares the Father's heart about our place as sons in His Family. Nothing is more important than *To Be Like Jesus*! ....#000605 $8.00

Prices are subject to change.

For a complete catalogue with current pricing, contact:

Engeltal Press

P.O. Box 447 • Jasper, ARK 72641 U.S.A.

Telephone (870) 446-2665 • Fax (870) 446-2259

Email books@eth-s.org

Website www.engeltalpress.com